HISTORICAL MAPS
OF THE
NAPOLEONIC WARS

HISTORICAL MAPS
OF THE
NAPOLEONIC WARS

SIMON FORTY AND MICHAEL SWIFT

BRASSEYS

Produced 2003 by

PRC Publishing Ltd,

64 Brewery Road, London N7 9NT

A member of **Chrysalis** Books plc

Published by Brasseys

64 Brewery Road, London N7 9NT

A member of **Chrysalis** Books plc

ISBN 1 85753 332 1

Printed and bound in China

Acknowledgments

The authors and publisher would like to thank the following for their assistance:
George Forty for his library; Paul Johnson and Hugh Alexander at the Public Record Office;
and Michael Bruff at Hampden Maps.

The maps credited to Hampden Maps below and many others can be purchased via
Hampden Maps' website at http://www.village-atlas.com.

For futher information, contact Hampden Maps at info@village-atlas.com.

Illustration credits

All the material in this book—unless credited below—is from the archives
of the Public Record Office, Kew.

Crown Copyright material in the Public Record Office is reproduced
by permission of the Controller of Her Majesty's Stationery Office.

Images are reproduced by courtesy of the Public Record Office.

George Forty Collection: p12, p19, p21, p22, p74 (both), p76, p80 (both), p87, p88, p90
(below), p92, p94 (left), p97 (left), p99 (both), p102, p103, p105, p110, p111, p112, p113,
p114, p115, p116, p117, p119 (right), p124, p125 (both), p126, p127, p132, p134, p135

Hampden Maps: p40 (both), p41, p53 (both), p64, p65, p66 (both), p67, p79 (both),
p100, p101, p118, p119

Bibliography

Caxton Pictorial Histories: *The Victory of Seapower*; *Winning the Napoleonic War
1806-1814*; Chatham Publishing, 1998.

Chandler, David: *The Campaigns of Napoleon*; Macmillan Publishing Co., Inc., 1966.

Chandler, David: *Waterloo The Hundred Days*; Osprey Publishing, 1997.

Cronin, Vincent: *Napoleon*; William Collins, 1971.

Duffy, Christopher: *Borodino Napoleon against Russia, 1812*; Sphere Books, 1972.

Haythornthwaite, Philip J.: *The Napoleonic Source Book*; Arms & Armour Press, 1990.

Haythornthwaite, Philip J.: *Who Was Who in the Napoleonic Wars*; Arms & Armour
Press, 1998.

Oman, Sir Charles: *A History of the Peninsular War* (7 vols.); Greenhill Books, 1996.

Paine, Lincoln: *Ships of the World. An Historical Encyclopedia*; Conway Maritime Press, 1998.

Pope, Stephen: *The Cassell Dictionary of Napoleonic Wars*; Cassell, 1999.

Smith, Digby: *Napoleon's Regiments*; Greenhill Books, 2000.

Warner, Richard: *Napoleon's Enemies*; Osprey Publishing, 1977.

CONTENTS

*INTRO*DUCTION

Prelude to a Revolution

The 18th century was one of considerable change and development. In many respects the period between 1700 and 1800 was critical in the creation of the modern age, marking the transition from the Renaissance and Reformation into the age of science and empire. It was the century when Europe continued to expand its knowledge of the unknown world and when philosophy and economics became more widely practised. It was also a century when many of the existing political regimes found themselves no longer strong enough to withstand the forces of reform. The century started with France at war with most of Europe and was to end in a similar vein; however, the nature of the two wars and the underlying tensions behind them were significantly different.

It was in the development of ideas in economics, science, and politics that the 18th century was crucial. Through writers like David Hume and Adam Smith, author of *Wealth of Nations*, the traditional view of economics radically changed. In philosophy, authors like Voltaire and Rousseau transformed the relationship between individual and state, while scientists like Joseph Priestley were fundamentally changing human understanding of the world and natural history. Allied with the growing European exploration of the planet came increasing scientific investigation of the world and its natural resources.

The 15th and 16th centuries had become known as the Renaissance because of the rebirth of art and literature; the 18th century was to become dominated by the Enlightenment—a belief in science, politics and economics. The old order—the so-called *ancien régime*—was under threat. In countries like Russia, under Catherine the Great, Prussia, under Frederick, and Austria, under Maria Theresa, the structures of the state gradually evolved into "Enlightened Despotism", with the monarchs tacitly adopting those reforms which they deemed appropriate, while never accepting true diminution of their power.

The logical extension of many of the philosophical developments of the 18th century was revolution, as the increased belief in the rights of man—as evinced so strongly in the writings of Tom Payne—were often incompatible with the existing order. Britain had, by the end of the 18th century, faced its revolution in its North American empire when the 13 Colonies revolted against George III demanding no taxation without representation. However, one country in Europe was perhaps both most ill-suited to face reform and also the one country where forces were present to make reform necessary—France.

The French Revolution

Although many of the most influential philosophers of the 18th century, such as Rousseau and Voltaire, were French, France itself was, ironically, among the most ill-prepared nations to face the political changes that were developing at the time.

During the course of the century, France's overseas ambitions in both North America and in India had been dealt serious blows by the British. In North America, following the Treaty of Paris in 1763 (consequent upon the Seven Years War), France had been forced to cede Quebec and its other territories on the mainland to Britain, while, in India, the British, under Clive and Hastings, had seen the power of the British East India Company expand dramatically, often at the expense of the French and their allies. In France, following the long reigns of Louis XIV and Louis XV (who succeeded to the throne in 1715 and was to reign until 1774), was the much weaker monarch Louis XVI and his much hated consort, the Austrian princess Marie Antoinette. The latter is, perhaps, best remembered for her quip "Let them eat cake" when she was informed about the poverty and hunger of much of the French population.

In the 15 years between his accession to the throne and the traditional date for the French Revolution, 1789, Louis XVI vacillated between unpopular ministers and policies as he sought desperately to restore the state's finances. One of the most influential ministers was Necker, in charge of finance from 1777 to 1781 and again in 1788, immediately prior to the Revolution. Ironically, during Necker's first period in control, the French allied themselves with the rebels in North America from 1777 onward in their campaign for independence from Britain. The rebels, espousing the cause of liberty and equality, would themselves find an echo back in France from 1789 onward as the *ancien régime* collapsed. The success of the Americans in casting off the colonial rule of King George III as well as the transmission of philosophical ideas between North American thinkers, such as Benjamin Franklin, and their European contemporaries, was crucial.

Just as the US Declaration of Independence in 1776 was the culmination of a period of increasing tension and political confusion, so too was the French Revolution. Although the actual revolution is commemorated to this day on 14 July, marking the storming of the notorious Bastille Prison in Paris, the period before that date was critical for the final disintegration of Louis XVI's rule. The pivotal moment, however, in France's drift to crisis came with the calling of the States General at Versailles in May 1789; the first time that this body had met for some 175 years. Notionally divided into three chambers, or Estates, the Third Estate—effectively the middle classes, under its president Jean Bailly—declared itself to be the National Assembly on 17 June 1789. The Third Estate demanded that the other two estates join it. Three days later, on 20 June, the Third Estate discovered that it had been locked out of its meeting chamber; transferring to an adjacent open hall, the members issued the Tennis Court Oath, binding them not to accept dissolution until a new constitution was agreed. A week later, Louis XVI instructed the other two estates to join with the Third Estate. However, fear that the king would attempt to subvert the assembly led to crowd trouble, culminating in the storming of the Bastille on 14 July and the capture of the king and royal family by the National Guard.

The following day the Commune de Paris was established under Jean Bailly as mayor in Paris. Among its first acts was the creation of a National Guard, under the Marquis de Lafayette (an aristocrat who had served with the rebels in the American War of Independence), which undermined the position of the king, yet further, guaranteeing that the reformers had some form of military backing. The pace of reform increased rapidly. On 4 August the National Assembly abolished all the remaining feudal rights of the nobility and on the 26th the National Assembly adopted the Declaration of the Rights of Man. The Declaration, based considerably on the American Declaration of Independence and heavily influenced by Benjamin Franklin (who was living in Paris), was to form the basis of the constitution of 1791. Although many of its rights were to be denied by later phases of the Revolution, it remained an important statement of liberal policies.

At this time Louis XIV remained at the palace of Versailles with his family, and it was to Versailles, on 5 October, that a march, primarily composed of women, headed to protest at the price of bread. It was as a result of this march that Marie Antoinette demonstrated her lack of understanding, which underlined both the detachment of the royal family from events as well as her own personal unpopularity.

It was during November that further reforms came. On the 2nd of the month, at the suggestion of the bishop of Autun, Charles-Maurice de Talleyrand, all church property was placed "at the disposal of the nation". Five days later the National Assembly forbade any member of the assembly from accepting public office under the king. On the 12th one of the most significant reforms occurred with the creation of the 80 administrative departments; these still form the basis of local government in France today.

France, however, was still a monarchy and, on 14 July 1790, on the first anniversary of the storming of the Bastille (an event marked by a large demonstration—La Fête de la Fédération) the king accepted the new constitution. In terms of what was to follow, 1790 represented the calm before the storm. However, there was a mutiny, suppressed by the army, at Nancy in August and the following month, Jacques Necker, one of the king's most able and trusted ministers, resigned.

Following the French Revolution, European powers were divided in their response to the events in Paris. Initially, there was much support, particularly among the intelligentsia, for the overthrow of a corrupt regime; however, even traditional reformers, like Edmund Burke in Britain, were by no means convinced that revolution would solve France's social inequalities. Burke, in his *Reflections on the French Revolution*, was one of the most articulate opponents of the revolution, although another Briton, Thomas Paine (arguably one of the most influential political thinkers of the late 18th century), was to argue cogently in favor of revolution in his book *The Rights of Man*.

However, it would be the response of the major states that would determine, ultimately, the fate of revolutionary France. In the build up to war, 1791 was to be a crucial year, marking as it did the collapse of

the immediate post-revolution settlement. The gradual drift toward a more extreme solution was shown both by the election of Honoré de Mirabeau (who could have been a figure to bring stability but who died three months later, aged 42) as president of the National Assembly on 29 January and by the fact that the mob prevented the king and his family moving to their chateau at St Cloud on 18 April. This latter event, which effectively showed that the monarch was a prisoner of the National Assembly, was to lead to one of the seminal events of the Revolution—the king's flight to Varennes.

De Mirabeau, who believed both in the monarchy but also the need for reform, is quoted as saying on his deathbed "I carry in my heart the funeral knell of the monarchy". He had recommended to the king, from the start, that the monarch should leave Paris and raise the royal standard in one of the more conservative parts of the country, possibly Rouen, where support could be gathered from the conservative Catholic, and monarchist forces that still existed. On 21 June 1791, the king, along with other members of the royal family and household, fled Paris, heading toward Metz where they hoped to meet up with forces under the Marquis de Bouillé. Progress was slow and, although recognized en route, the party was allowed to reach Varennes where, again recognized, this time, the peasants refused to allow them through. Bouillé's forces failed to rescue the monarch and the party was returned to Paris in ignominy, arriving back at the palace of the Tuileries on 25 June. Although the royal family were now more firmly prisoners than before, the National Assembly still sought to achieve a constitution with the monarch at its head and thus required Louis's consent to any new constitution.

However, events outside Paris were now starting to influence the position. On 6 July 1791 Leopold II, the Holy Roman Emperor, issued the Padia Circular. In this he called for support for Louis against the National Assembly. On the same day, in Koblenz, the Count d'Artois made the city the headquarters of the nobles exiled from France—the so-called émigrés. A month later, on 27 August, the Prussian and Habsburg monarchs issued the Declaration of Pillnitz, by which they stated that they would intervene in France to ensure the restoration of the monarchy with the support of other nations. The British Prime Minister, William Pitt the Younger, refused to back the declaration, stat-ing that Britain would remain neutral in any war over the Revolution. In this Pitt was reflecting British ambivalence over events in France; on the one hand, the establishment was concerned that radical action could cross the Channel, while on the other there was sympathy among many of the leading politicians for the aspirations of the reform-ers. Inevitably, France saw the declaration as an immediate threat. On 3 September the National Assembly ratified the new constitution, trans-forming the country into a constitutional monarchy. Ten days later, France annexed Avignon, a territory held by the Papacy since the 14th century. On the last day of September, the National Assembly was dis-solved to make way for a new Legislative Assembly, which first met the following month. However, one of the National Assembly's final acts was to bar members from being elected to its replacement. This had one critical result: many of the experienced reformers that had influ-enced the creation of the new constitution were now debarred from influencing the new body.

Given the increasing threat from outside, it was no surprise that one faction of the new assembly, the republican Girondists—led by Brissot, Roland, his wife, Pétion, and Vergniaud—demanded an immediate war against Austria. At this stage, war did not result, but it was clear evi-dence that European stability was under threat. The monarch, despite his position, still had some influence; on 9 November, for example, he vetoed a decree from the assembly demanding, on pain of death, the return of the émigrés from abroad.

A number of events in early 1792 led inexorably to war. On 7 February 1792 Austria and Prussia formed an alliance. On 1 March, Francis II succeeded Leopold II both as Habsburg monarch and, in July, as Holy Roman Emperor. On 23 March, the Girondists under Jean Roland and Charles-François Dumouriez, came to power; a month later, on 20 April, France declared war on Austria as the latter refused to repudiate treaties threatening French national security. This was fol-lowed, on 8 July 1792, by the French declaration of war against Prussia. A fortnight later, on 25 July 1792, the Duke of Brunswick, Karl Wilhelm, declared that Paris would be destroyed by Prussian forces if the French royal family was harmed.

Domestically, the situation was fast deteriorating for the king and his family. On 20 June 1792, before the Prussian ultimatum, the Paris mob had stormed the Tuileries Palace in response to the king's rejection of laws passed by the Legislative Assembly, but this was to be a mere side-show to the mob's response in August, once it became aware that an Austro-Prussian army, commanded by the Duke of Brunswick, had invaded France. Brunswick had 42,000 Prussians, 29,000 Austrians ands 6,000 Hessians under his command; normally, this would have been considered an insufficient force to invade France, but these were atypical circumstances. On 19 July he invaded, breaching the French armies located at Sedan and Metz before heading toward the fortress at Longwy. However, as a result of poor supply and hostility, progress was slow and Longwy was not reached until 20 August. After a short siege, the fortress surrendered and Brunswick's army moved toward Verdun on 26 August; it surrendered on 2 September—Paris was now under serious threat.

In Paris, events were moving quickly. On 10 August, the mob again stormed the Tuileries Palace, massacring his guards and the King's authority was suspended by the Assembly. A new Commune de Paris was established, replacing that created in 1789, and government was now in the hands of this and the Assembly. Two days later, the king and the royal family were imprisoned. News that Verdun had fallen, along with the fact that Lafayette had fled to the Austrians on 19 August (after his failure to lead an army to Paris in order to suppress the worst excesses of the revolution), led to panic in Paris. Between 2 and 6 September 1792, more than 1,400 prisoners were massacred—ironically most were common criminals rather than the anticipated counter-revolutionaries—as the cry went up that the enemy was at the gate and that Paris was full of suspected fifth columnists eager to overturn the revolution.

Militarily, although the Legislative Assembly was slow to react to the invasion, the position was to improve dramatically on 20 September, when Brunswick's forces were defeated at the Battle of Valmy by French forces under Charles-François Dumouriez and François Kellerman. There were a number of factors in Brunswick's defeat. Firstly, the French artillery had been much improved by the influence of Gribeauval and had better quality gunpowder. Secondly, although part of the French army comprised volunteers, the bulk of it was composed of experienced officers, many of whom had recently experienced war by serving in the US War of Independence. In contrast, the Prussian forces, although numerous, were ill-experienced. Although the battle was technically inconclusive, the strategic advantage lay with the French, as Brunswick's position saw him with a severed supply line to Verdun. As a result, he retreated back toward the German border. French forces allowed Brunswick to escape eastward; their greater target was to attack Austrian interests in Belgium.

Back in Paris, at the same time as Brunswick was being defeated, the Legislative Assembly continued the process of reform, dissolving religious orders and instituting civil marriage and divorce. These were, however, to be the last acts of the Assembly; it was replaced on 21 September by the National Convention. The following day the monarchy was abolished; France became a republic.

In November, the Girondist government fell, to be replaced by the Jacobins under Georges Danton and, on 19 November, the National Convention sought to export revolution when it proclaimed its support for any population seeking to overthrow their government. The potency of revolution became explicit early in December, when, on the 5th of the month, a revolution, although short-lived, occurred in Geneva.

Simultaneous with the revolution in Geneva, in Paris the trial of the king commenced. It had been occasioned by the discovery at the Tuileries of correspondence between the royal family and the Austrians but was also to be useful in terms of the infighting between the various revolutionary factions and was, ultimately, to be one of the causes of the disgrace of the Girondists since, if they opposed either the trial or the likely penalty, they could be denounced as either traitors or monarchists. The trial itself was a foregone conclusion; the king was found guilty and by a majority of one was sentenced to death. An attempt to delay the execution or to grant clemency was defeated and, on 21 January 1793, the king was executed by guillotine.

The Early Phases of the War

Following Brunswick's defeat, French forces moved on to the offensive. During September, the country occupied Savoy and Nice in the

south, formally annexing Savoy two months later. In early October, forces under General Adam de Custine, in pursuit of Brunswick, crossed the Rhine and captured the city of Mainz on 19 October. Habsburg power in the Austrian Netherlands—as Belgium was then known—was destroyed on 6 November 1792 when a French army under Dumouriez defeated the Austrians at the Battle of Jemappes and occupied Brussels.

The execution of the king outraged many in Europe, including a number of those who had previously been sympathetic to the French. On 1 February 1793 the French declared war on Britain and the Dutch Republic, which was followed by a declaration of war on Spain the following month. Britain's first response to the French declaration was to sign a treaty with Russia banning all Baltic trade with France. And, on 11 March, William Pitt initiated a policy of issuing Exchequer bills to fund the subsidy of potential allies in the war with France—Britain had traditionally waged war in Europe through funding of allies rather than possessing a large standing army for deployment—and to improve domestic defense.

Following the French declaration of war, Spain invaded the territories of Navarre and Roussillon, on the border, on 7 March 1793. Elsewhere the war also started to go against the French. In the Austrian Netherlands, Dumouriez was defeated on 18 March at the Battle of Neerwinden by the Austrian army led by Friedrich Josias, Prince of Saxe-Coburg. The defeat resulted in the Austrians regaining control of Belgium and, on 5 April, Dumouriez defected to the Austrians. With the Holy Roman Empire having declared war against France on 26 March, revolutionary France was now in conflict with all the major powers of Western Europe.

Domestic Turmoil

Just as the war started to go against the French, so the domestic situation in France continued to deteriorate after the execution of Louis XVI. In the pro-monarchist region of La Vendée, conservative forces launched a rebellion against Paris, which was to continue until later in the year. However, although their failure to capture Granville, near

Cherbourg, meant that the British were unable to come to their aid and the rebels were defeated at the Battle of Cholet on 17 October 1793—and, finally at the Battle of Le Mans on 12 December. On the day following the defeat at Neerwinden, a new body—the Committee of Public Safety—was established in Paris led by the Jacobin, Georges Danton. Six weeks later the committee was joined by another leading revolutionary, Louis St-Just.

The threat to the republic was all too real in much of France. In Lyon, where trade in the silk industry had collapsed, the National Guard revolted in May and the rebels were joined by those who fled Paris on 2 June following the arrest of the surviving Girondists. The rebels imprisoned the mayor and massacred some 20 local Jacobins. The port of Toulon revolted and was handed over to the British under Admiral Sir Samuel Hood by royalists on 28 August. The revolt in Lyon was to continue until October when the central government reclaimed the city; the rebels fled or were massacred, while the city itself was ordered to be destroyed. In December 1793 Toulon finally surrendered; one factor in its defeat was the heavy bombardment engineered by a young officer, Napoleon Bonaparte, who would become one of the pivotal figures of the period.

The military failure, highlighted by the treason of Dumouriez, was to lead to the fall of the Girondists on 2 June 1793 when their leader, Jacques Brissot, was arrested. The ultimate triumph of the Jacobins resulted in the period known as 'The Terror'. The Committee of Public Safety, under Marie-Jean Hérault de Séchelles, introduced a new constitution on 24 June; this allowed for a single legislative chamber and for universal male suffrage.

The immediate trigger for the Terror was the assassination of Jean Paul Marat, a leading member of the Jacobin faction. On 13 July 1793 he was stabbed to death, while in his bath, by a 25-year-old aristocrat, Charlotte Corday. In a macabre demonstration, his body was exhibited to the crowd on the following day and the reaction was swift. The imprisonment of all suspects was ordered and representatives traveled far and wide to hunt down potential counter-revolutionaries while, at the same time, enforcing conscription on all unmarried men aged between 18 and 25 for military service. In certain parts of France the Terror was relatively limited; elsewhere, vast numbers were to meet a bloody end. In Paris, the guillotine was to see Marie Antoinette executed in October 1793 and, on 31 October, 21 leading Girondists, including Brissot and Vergniaud, were executed in a single day after a show trial. Other leading Girondists, such as Roland, Condorcet and Pétion, escaped a similar fate by committing suicide.

One of the Jacobin leaders of the Terror was Maximilien-Françoise Robespierre, who had joined the Committee of Public Safety on 27 July, becoming its effective leader.

Military Successes and Domestic Strife

While the domestic situation continued to deteriorate, on the battlefield French forces began to reverse some of the earlier setbacks. Prussian forces under the Duke of Brunswick captured Mainz on 23 July 1793 and forced French troops to leave Germany while British forces landed at Toulon in August. However, on 6 September a new French offensive, led by General Jean Houchard, was launched in Belgium and a British army, led by the Duke of York, was defeated at the Battle of Hondschoote.

Within France, the second half of 1793 saw victory over the rebels in La Vendée and at Lyon as well as the expulsion of the British from Toulon. This was followed by General Louis Hoche's victory over the Austrian forces under General Dagobert Würmser at Weissenberg, Alsace, on 26 December. This victory forced the Austrians once again to retreat over the Rhine.

However, domestically the power struggle within the various revolutionary factions continued. On 4 March the leader of the sans-culottes—the Paris mob—Jacques Hébert demanded a revolution against Georges Danton. Although Hébert was unsuccessful in his campaign, Danton's position had been compromised and both he and Camille Desmoulins were to fall victim to Robespierre's ambitions and the ongoing Terror, being executed by guillotine on 5 April 1794. Two months later, on 10 June, the Law of the 22 Prairial was passed; this increased the power of the tribunals and resulted in a further wave of mass executions. In addition, the conventional calendar was replaced by a new one, based on dating from the start of the Revolution.

On 19 April 1794 the British and Prussians signed the Treaty of the Hague, under which Britain agreed to fund 60,000 Dutch and Prussian troops in the war against France; again Britain's policy was to subsidize mercenaries in Europe while actively fighting the war at sea. Thus, on 1 June 1794, the Royal Navy under Lord Howe defeated the French fleet in the Battle of the Glorious First of June in the English Channel, near Brest. On land, however, the French were more successful. On 18 May 1794, the French, under Charles Pichegru, defeated a combined British and Austrian army under Friedrich Josias at Tourcoing, in northwest France. This was followed with the capture of Charleroi, the Austrian Netherlands, on 25 June. The following day, Friedrich Josias, who had been defeated at Charleroi the previous day, was again defeated, this time by Jean-Baptiste Jourdan's army at Fleurus. As a result, Austrian forces retreated from Belgium. Further south, French forces invaded the Spanish border districts of Catalonia and Guipúzcoa in June 1794, while four months later a northern army under Jean Moreau reached the Rhine once again.

Domestically, the tide, however, had turned against the ambitious Robespierre. On 27/28 July—9 Thermidor—a conspiracy led by moderates resulted in the fall of Robespierre and the abolition of the Paris Commune; both Robespierre and Louis St-Just were executed. This heralded the onset of a new phase of the Revolution—Moderate Republicanism—which lasted until October 1795. With the fall of Robespierre and the closure of the Jacobin Club (on 11 November 1794 as a result of attacks by anti-revolutionary forces—the "*jeunesse dorée*"), the revolution reverted to the more liberal principles of the early days despite the opposition of the Paris Mob. The new constitution that resulted—the third—was approved by the Convention on 22 August 1795. This constitution allowed for the country to be governed by a bicameral parliament with an executive "Directory" of five. It was the Directory that took the reins of power in November 1795. The new constitution faced insurrection when, on 5 October 1795, rebel royalists attempted to seize power in the Revolt of 13 Vendémiaire. The revolt was crushed by Barras and Bonaparte; the latter's stout defense of the revolution helped bring him to greater prominence.

By the time the Directory came to power, the military situation had largely been resolved. On 25 October 1794 Prussia ceased hostilities;

this was followed in December by both Prussia and Spain seeking peace with France and, on the 27th of the month, by Pichegru's army invading the Dutch Republic. On 19 January Pichegru occupied Amsterdam, capturing the Dutch fleet at Texel, and the rest of the country soon followed. French control over the Dutch Republic was now total; on 16 May the country, now known as the Batavian Republic, signed an alliance with France. On 9 February 1795, Tuscany made peace with France while, on 15 February, the final royalist supporters in La Vendée made peace with the republic in the Peace of La Jaunae. On 5 April, Prussia and France signed the Treaty of Basel, which recognized French territorial gains up to the west bank of the Rhine, while also confirming the strengthened Prussian position to the east. French influence in the Low Countries was further strengthened on 25 June 1795 when Luxembourg surrendered.

On 27 June 1795, the British launched a second incursion onto the French mainland in support of pro-monarchist groups and backed by *émigrés* who had earlier fled to Britain, when a force landed at Quiberon, in Brittany. However, this invasion was short-lived and quickly defeated by a French force under Lazard Hoche. A month later, on 27 July, France signed a peace treaty with Spain. In early September, the French suffered a minor military setback when Austrian forces under Archduke Charles defeated Jean-Baptise Jourdan along the east bank of the Rhine. However, later in the month Jourdan's forces again crossed the river and, on 20 September, Pichegru occupied Mannheim. On 1 October, French control over the Austrian Netherlands became formal through annexation. And, on 24 November, the French forces under Barthélemy Schérer defeated the Austrians at the Battle of Loano in northern Italy.

The Directory

The new regime in Paris came to power on 4 November 1795 with war continuing against the Austrians in Europe and against Britain in the West Indies.

On 13 April 1796, Bonaparte, who had married Joséphine de Beauharnais (widow of an aristocrat) on 9 March 1796, took command of the French forces in Italy. His appointment resulted in immediate success with victory over the Piedmontese at Mondivo on 22 April. Later the same month, the threat posed by Napoleon forced the Sardinians to break their alliance with Austria. Napoleon's success continued unabated: on 10 May 1795 his army defeated the Austrians at Lodi and, on 15 May, French forces entered Milan. On the same day, the Kingdom of Sardinia signed the Treaty of Cherasco with France, by which Savoy and Nice were ceded to France. The following day, Lombardy was declared a republic under French rule.

Further north, along the Rhine, the French initially suffered a reverse in June 1796, after an invasion of Franconia by Jourdan, when the army was forced to retreat. But the position was reversed later in the month when a second French force, under Victor Moreau, also crossed in Franconia, in order to link up with Jourdan and push toward Austria. However, Jourdan's army was defeated by the Austrians under Archduke Charles at Amberg on 29 August 1796 and Charles scored a second major victory at Würzburg on 3 September over Jourdan; the defeat caused the French commander to resign.

While the French were suffering setbacks in Germany, in Italy, Napoleon's position continued to improve. On 15 August, his army defeated an Austrian force led by Count Dagobert Würmser at Castiglione Delle Stiviere. This victory prevented the Austrians from relieving the besieged city of Mantua. On 16 October, French control of much of Italy was reflected in Napoleon's creation of the Cisalpine Republic, a client state dominated by France, that incorporated the Papal States of Bologna and Ferrara along with the Duchy of Modena. A month later, on 15 November, Napoleon inflicted a further defeat on the Austrians, this time with victory over Joseph Alvintzi at Arcole.

Just as French military might was starting to achieve considerable success, so France itself began to emerge from its post-Revolution status of pariah. On 19 August, at San Ildefonso, an alliance was agreed between France and Spain; these traditional allies, which had both been ruled by branches of the Bourbon family (as indeed Spain still was), had been united earlier in the 18th century in their opposition to Britain's colonial expansion in North America. One immediate consequence of the alliance was that the Royal Navy abandoned the Mediterranean for strategic reasons in November 1796.

Although, generally, the year had proved positive for the French there had been one major setback. For the British, Ireland represented an Achilles' heel and the French sought to exploit it when, in December, it launched an invasion of Ireland at Bantry Bay. Inspired by the Irish Protestant revolutionary, Wolfe Tone, the French sent 43 ships and 15,000 men under Lazare Hoche. However, the attack proved ill-judged, with disagreements over the point of landing and storms causing the fleet to be separated, and was quickly abandoned. Britain, however, only possessed 11,000 men in Ireland at the time and, had the invasion proceeded, history might have been different. For Hoche, it represented one of his last military acts; he was to die the following year. For the French, it was a slightly curious act, given the fact they were in peace discussions with the British, although these negotiations were to fail.

The new year, 1797, started with more success for Bonaparte when he emerged victorious, in the Battle of Rivoli on 4 January, over the Austrians under Alvintzi. This was followed, on 2 February, by the surrender of the Duchy of Mantua. A fortnight later, on 16 February, the Pope, Pius VI, formally ceded Bologna, Romagna, and Ferrara to France under the Treaty of Tolentino. Napoleon's army now headed northward through the Tyrol toward the Austrian capital of Vienna. The threat to its homeland forced the Austrians to peace, with a preliminary settlement being agreed at Leoben, in Austria, on 18 April. The peace with Austria was confirmed on 17 October 1798 by the Treaty of Campo Formio. This came shortly after Napoleon had further strengthened the French position in Italy by creating the Ligurian Republic based in Genoa, on 6 June, and by the capture of the Ionian Islands, on 28 June. Through this treaty, France gained the Ionian Islands while Austria gained Venice and its associated lands of Dalmatia and Istria. The French-dominated republics of Cisalpine and Liguria were also recognized, as was French rule over the Austrian Netherlands. It was also

Napoleon Bonaparte was born in Ajaccio, Corsica, in 1769. He went to military schools at Brienne and Paris before becoming an artillery officer in 1785. Promoted quickly, by 1793 he was a brigadier, by 1796 commander of the Army of Italy, by 1800 first consul and on 16 May 1804 Emperor of France.

agreed that a separate treaty, to be debated at Rastatt, in Germany, would also be negotiated between France and the Holy Roman Empire. The Rastatt Conference opened on 16 December, but was to break up without agreement on 8 April 1799.

Settlement with Austria effectively meant that Britain now stood alone against the French. Traditionally, Britain had relied upon its seapower to thwart potential invaders, but two mutinies—at Spithead, on 15 April, and the Nore, on 2 May—showed that discontent was rife even within Britain's forces. Both mutinies were suppressed quickly, the latter seeing its leader, Richard Parker, hung from the yard-arm. Although Britain and France held peace negotiations at Lille, in the period between October and December 1797, these came to nothing; clearly the French had not expected much from the talks as, during this period, Napoleon, fresh from his triumphs in Italy, was appointed commander of a proposed invasion force of the British Isles.

In the Low Countries and in Central and Southern Europe, French influence—either direct or indirect—continued to increase. On 22 January 1798 a Directory-based government was established in the Batavian Republic and, two days later, the Lemanic Republic was declared in Geneva. On 11 February French forces occupied Rome and, four days later, the Roman Republic was declared despite the opposition of the Pope, who went into exile at Valence, in France. On 29 March, the Helvetian Republic was proclaimed by pro-French revolutionaries in Switzerland and, on 26 April, the French annexed Geneva. The scene was now set for one of the great military adventures of the period.

Napoleon and Egypt

On 19 May 1798 the French invasion force left Toulon under the command of Napoleon. Apart from the military force, Napoleon also had on board numerous savants whose task it was to explore and record the history and artefacts of ancient Egypt as the invasion progressed. The end of the 18th century had witnessed a great explosion in interest in the history and language of ancient Egypt and the French expedition was to play a crucial role in the ultimate discovery of much of ancient

Egypt's history. It was particularly crucial in terms of deciphering the hieroglyphs.

The first action that the invasion fleet saw was the conquest of the island of Malta, which was occupied on 12 June. Until this point, the island had been under the control of the Knights of St John, of whom Tsar Paul I of Russia was the Grand Master. From there the French sailed eastward, reaching Egypt the following month. After capturing Alexandria, Napoleon's forces defeated the Marmalukes to establish control of the land at the Battle of the Pyramids on 21 July 1798. However, while Napoleon was engaged ashore, a Royal Navy fleet, which had been chasing the French fleet across the Mediterranean, came upon the French ships in Aboukir Bay. Under Horatio Nelson, the Royal Navy achieved a great victory at the Battle of the Nile, with the result that the French land forces were cut off in Egypt and the Royal Navy achieved supremacy in the Mediterranean.

Despite this setback, Napoleon continued to consolidate French power in the Middle East. In January 1799 the French advanced into the Turkish province of Syria—the Turks having declared war on France in September 1798 and having signed an anti-French alliance with Britain and Russia. On 2 March 1799, the French army started to besiege Acre, which was defended by Turkish troops alongside a small British detachment under Sydney Smith. The siege was, however, unsuccessful and the French forces withdrew on 20 May. Two months later, Napoleon gained another victory, defeating a Turkish army at Aboukir on 24 July, but this effectively marked the end of Napoleon's career in Egypt; on 22 August he returned to take command of French forces in Europe, arriving back at Fréjus on 9 October 1799.

Although Napoleon had returned to France, French military action in Egypt continued. On 20 March 1800, the French, commanded by Jean Baptiste Kléber, defeated the Ottoman army at Heliopolis and, after the victory, marched toward Cairo, with the intention of restoring French control over the country. Three months later, however, on 14 June, Kléber was assassinated just as he assumed power.

On 8 March 1801, British forces, under William Keith, landed at Aboukir with the intention of removing French influence from Egypt. On 21 March, the French army in Egypt was defeated by the British under Abercromby near Alexandria. On 27 June 1801, the British captured Cairo from its French occupiers. On 2 September all French forces in Egypt, under the command of Jean Menou, surrendered to the British and were granted safe passage home.

The Directory's Last Year

Although the 1796 invasion of Ireland had proved unsuccessful, a further opportunity arose two years later. On 23 May 1798 a revolt led by the United Irish movement, allied with some elements within the Catholic population, broke out. This revolt, however, was short-lived, being suppressed finally by the victory of Lord Lake at the Battle of Vinegar Hill, County Wexford, on 21 June. Although the revolt had started out with no sectarian agenda, during the period atrocities were committed against the population of both sects and, as a result, many anti-British Protestants changed allegiance, thereby setting a pattern that persists to this day. It has been estimated that some 30,000 were killed during the summer's insurrection.

Shortly after the defeat of the rebels, a small French force of some 1,200 men commanded by Jean Humbert landed at Killala Bay with the intention of backing the rebels. However, it was a case of too little, too late, and, after two months, the surviving French force surrendered at Balinasloe on 27 October. Among those captured was Wolfe Tone, who had been seized while with a small French fleet in Lough Swilly in September 1798 and who was to commit suicide while awaiting execution for treason. Among the consequences of the two failed French invasions was the Act of Union of 1801, which transferred the government of Ireland from Dublin to London.

In mainland Europe, on 19 August 1799 the French signed a formal alliance with the Helvetian Republic and, on 5 September, at the suggestion of Jourdan, conscription was introduced to France. In Italy, the kingdom of Piedmont was occupied by French forces commanded by Barthélemy-Catherine Joubert during November 1798 and, on 29 November, King Ferdinand IV of Naples declared war on France. On 4 December the French reciprocated the Neapolitan declaration and—after forcing King Charles Emanuel of Sardinia to abdicate, on 9 December, and recapturing Rome from the Austrians under Karl Mack

von Lieberich, on the 15th—invaded the Kingdom of Naples. On 24 December an alliance was formed between Britain and Russia, soon to be joined by Turkey; this was the basis of the "Second Coalition" against France. The actual coalition, which included Britain, Russia, Portugal, Naples, and the Ottoman Empire, was formalized under the aegis of William Pitt the Younger, the British Prime Minister, on 1 June 1799.

On 8 February, the French position in Naples was threatened by a revolt led by Cardinal Fabrizio Ruffo, the papal vicar-General to the Kingdom of Naples; by June, such was his success, that he recaptured Naples from the French army. Elsewhere, the French position was also under threat; on 1 March 1799, a joint Russo-Turkish force captured the Ionian Islands and, on 12 March, despite the earlier peace treaty, Austria declared war. The Austrians achieved an immediate military victory when, on 25 March, their army under the command of Archduke Charles defeated a French force under Jourdan at Stockach, although this defeat was countered in Italy by the occupation of Tuscany on the same day by French forces.

However, on 5 April and on 27 April, the French suffered two reverses in Italy when the army under Schérer was defeated at Magnano by the Austrian army under Paul von Kray, and when Moreau was defeated by a joint Russo-Austrian force under Count Alexander Vasilyevich Suvorov at the Battle of Cassano. As a result of the latter defeat, Turin fell to Suvorov. Further setbacks occurred on 4 June 1799, when the French under André Massena were defeated by Archduke Charles at Zurich, and on 17-19 June, when Suvorov defeated the French governor of Rome (Jacques-Alexander MacDonald) at the Battle of the Trebbia. The French force was marching to relieve Moreau at Genoa. A further defeat occurred on 15 August when Suvorov defeated the French under Joubert at Novi. During the battle the French commander was killed and the anti-French forces were able, as a result of the victory, to head across the Alps toward France.

It was not only in Italy that the French were threatened. On 13 September the Duke of York took command of a combined British and Russian army in the Batavian Republic (Netherlands) with the intention of liberating both it and the Austrian Netherlands; however, his force was to be defeated on 19 June by the French and Batavian army at the Battle of Bergen-op-Zoom. On 18 October, the Duke of York sur-

rendered with his Russian and British army at Alkmaar. The British reaction to this setback was to declare, on 21 November 1799, that the entire coast of the Batavian Republic was to be blockaded. To the south, the position was also improved by the victory of Massena over the Russian army under Korsakov at the Battle of Zurich, on 25-27 September, when the French position was strengthened by the inability of Suvorov to reach the battle with the main Russian army. Defeated, the Russians retreated and Austrian forces under Archduke Charles also fell back. The Russian defeats resulted, on 22 October, in their renunciation of the treaty with Austria.

This, therefore, was the military position in the last days of the Directory when Napoleon returned from Egypt.

The End of the Directory

While there had been some changes of personnel during the life of the Directory, it had also represented a period of some domestic stability at home and some military success abroad. However, toward the end of its four-year rule, internal dissent and military defeat resulted in its growing unpopularity and paved the way for Bonaparte's *coup d'état* of 18 Brumaire (9 November). The coup was achieved by summoning the two parliamentary chambers—the Council of the Ancients and the Council of the Five Hundred—to St Cloud, a small town north of Paris, where, intimidated by the army of Napoleon and Murat, they nominated three consuls—Napoleon, Sieyès, and Ducos—to replace the five Directors before being dispersed. The change of regime was confirmed by the Constitution of the Year VIII. This new constitution, confirmed on 25 December 1799, allowed for three Consuls, of whom Napoleon was the First. As First Consul, Napoleon moved into the Tuileries Palace on 19 February 1800.

While events in Paris unfolded, militarily the position saw Russia leave its coalition with Austria on 22 October 1799 and the Austrians occupy the March of Ancona on the Adriatic coast of Italy. One of Napoleon's first acts was to offer peace to both Austria and Britain, but his overtures were rejected. The French military position improved in early 1800 when, on 17 January, the Treaty of Montluçon ended the royalist rebellion in La Vendée and freed French troops to fight against Austria, whose army, from April 1800, was under the control of Paul von Kray.

In his first major engagement, von Kray was defeated by the French army under Victor Moreau at the Battle of Biberach, near Württemberg in Germany, on 9 May 1800. Later that month, between the 15th and the 20th, a French army, with Napoleon at its head, crossed the Great St Bernard Pass en route to Italy, with the intention of restoring French control. On 2 June, the French, under Joachim Murat, recaptured Milan and, a fortnight later, on 16 June, Napoleon's army defeated the Austrians, under Michel Melas, at the Battle of Marengo. The Austrian defeat ensured French control was restored over Italy and allowed Napoleon to offer the Duke of Parma, son-in-law to the King of Spain, the title of King of Tuscany. The Austrians' position deteriorated further when Moreau defeated the Austrian army under Archduke John at Hohenlinden on 3 December 1800.

Militarily, the only major setback that the French suffered during 1800 was the loss of the island of Malta to the British on 5 September. Elsewhere, the northern European states of Russia and Sweden, later to be joined by Russia (on 3 March 1801) and Denmark (on 27 February 1801), agreed on the second Armed Neutrality of the North on 16 December. The first Armed Neutrality had existed between 1780 and the following year to ensure rights of neutral shipping during the American War of Independence; its recreation in 1800 represented a diplomatic triumph for France, which saw it as a means of breaking the British blockade. However, the only nation with a navy capable of enforcing the principle was Denmark, whose fleet was effectively destroyed by Nelson in the battle of Copenhagen on 2 April 1801. Along with the French, Denmark had attempted to close the River Elbe by occupying the free city of Hamburg. Without the Danish fleet, Armed Neutrality was ineffective and it failed by the end of 1801, following the Treaty of St Petersburg on 17 June 1801 between Britain, Prussia, and Russia, which recognized Britain's right to search merchant vessels. The treaty was followed on 19 June by a maritime convention between Britain and Russia. Denmark signed the Treaty of St Petersburg on 23 October 1801 to be followed by Sweden on 30 March 1802.

Domestically, Napoleon's position was strengthened at the end of the year when, following the discovery of a plot against him, he was able to send a number of republicans into exile to a French colony in South America. Improved relations with Spain followed on 29 January 1801 when two countries agreed to attempt to pressurize Portugal by ultimatum to break the latter's long allegiance to Britain. This was formalized on 21 March 1801 by the Treaty of Aranjuez. By this treaty, the Spaniards agreed to cede the territory of Louisiana in north America to France; this territory was sold to the United States of America along with New Orleans on 30 April 1803 for some $27 million.

On 9 March 1801 the French defeat of Austria was marked by the Treaty of Lunéville. This effectively dismembered the Holy Roman Empire, ceding all territory west of the Rhine to France and transferring Tuscany to the Duchy of Parma in order to create the new kingdom of Etruria. The treaty also recognized the Batavian, Cisalpine, Helvetian, and Ligurian republics.

A second treaty, the Peace of Florence, was signed between France and the Kingdom of Naples on 28 March 1801. This resulted in British ships being excluded from Neapolitan ports. In early April 1801, Hanover—the part of Germany ruled over by the British monarch George III as Elector—was occupied by Prussian troops. In the Iberian peninsula, Spain achieved its objectives against Portugal in a brief war, which was settled by the Treaty of Badajoz, signed on 6 June 1801, and confirmed by the Portuguese/French Treaty of Madrid, signed on 29 September, in which Portugal renounced its alliance with Britain, ceded the province of Olivenza to Spain, and closed its ports to British ships. At sea, however, the Royal Navy continued to ensure some success for the anti-French forces, with victory for Admiral James Saumarez against the joint Spanish/French fleet at Algerciras on 12 July 1801.

By this date, however, the various combatant nations were beginning to feel the strain of war and, during early October, negotiations commenced between Britain and France for a peace treaty. This treaty envisaged the return of a number of British colonial conquests (excluding Ceylon and Trinidad) to the French, Spanish, and Dutch; agreed that both Britain and France were to leave Egypt, which would be restored to Ottoman rule; offered independence to the Ionian Islands;

Portuguese security; and French withdrawal from the Papal States and Naples. The Treaty of Amiens came into effect on 27 March 1802, bringing peace to Europe.

The year of 1802 proved to be relatively quiet, although there were a number of other significant developments. On 26 January Napoleon became President of the Cisalpine Republic. On 29 June, Genoa agreed a new constitution, which made it subservient to France. On 26 August, France seized the island of Elba, which had been abandoned by Britain five years earlier and on 21 September the duchy of Piedmont was incorporated into France. On the domestic front, on 2 August, Napoleon became First Consul for life and this was followed, a fortnight later, by the Fifth Constitution (Constitution of Year XII), which enhanced further Napoleon's position and reduced the power of Tribune, while enhancing the position of the Senate.

War Resumes

Despite the Treaty of Amiens, hostility remained between Britain and France, partly over the latter's continuing interference in the internal affairs of Switzerland and Italy and partly as a result of Britain's refusal to return Malta to the Knights of St John.

War resumed on 16 May 1803 and the following day Britain placed an embargo on all French and Dutch boats in British ports. On 1 June 1803 the French invaded Hanover and, on 15 July, a camp was established at Boulogne for an army intended by Napoleon to spearhead the invasion of Britain. This was supplemented, on 23 August, by two further camps at St Omer, in France, and Bruges, in Belgium. Simultaneously, work began on constructing the fleet required to ship the men and equipment across the Channel.

Despite the military build up, however, there was no invasion; indeed, the following year saw relatively little military action as both sides gradually sought to build alliances for the future. There were a number of significant events during the year, none the less. On 16 May 1804 Napoleon was proclaimed emperor and was crowned on 2 December in Paris with the Pope, Pius VII, officiating; this brought to an end the first Republic in France. On 6 November Francis II of Austria

signed a secret treaty with Russia to oppose any further French interference in Italy; this was followed five days later by a joint Russian and Austrian agreement to support the Ottoman empire against any French attack in the Balkans or Middle East. On 12 December, Spain came into the war on France's side, declaring war against Britain.

As with other phases of the war, much of Britain's primary action was at sea. Between April and July 1805, the Royal Navy under Nelson pursued a French-Spanish fleet under Pierre Villeneuve to the West Indies and back, but was unable to draw the fleet into action. However, a small engagement did occur on 22 July when a British detachment under Robert Calder defeated Villeneuve near Cape Finisterre, northern Spain. Although two French ships were captured, Villeneuve escaped with the bulk of his fleet to Cadiz.

Elsewhere, the anti-French coalition was gradually being created. On 11 April, Britain and Russia sign the Treaty of St Petersburg, creating the Third Coalition. Under the treaty Britain agreed to help finance the Russian military effort. The treaty envisaged the liberation of the northern German states and Italy, the protection of the Netherlands and Switzerland, and the removal of French domination from Naples. On 9 August, Austria joined Britain, Russia, and Sweden as a member of the coalition. With Austria now ranged against him, Napoleon's tactics changed; from late August onward he transferred the army—sitting in northern France and Belgium for the planned invasion of Britain—to the Austrian front. This move was prudent as, on 8 September, the Austrian army under Karl Mack von Leiberich invaded Bavaria and marched to Ulm on the Danube. However, Napoleon surprised von Leiberich by an outflanking maneuver, forcing the Austrians to surrender on 20 October with 30,000 being captured. The French military successes in Europe continued on 2 December with the crushing defeat of the joint Russian and Austrian army at Austerlitz. The defeat at Austerlitz resulted in the collapse of the anti-French coalition. Prussia, not a combatant at this stage, signed the Treaty of Schönbrunn on 15 December. By this Prussia ceded Cleves, Neuchâtel, and Ansbach to the French, while gaining control of Hanover. More significant was the Treaty of Pressburg, signed on 26 December, between Austria and France, by which Austria recognized French control in Italy and renounced its territories in Italy, the Tyrol and southern Germany—

thereby allowing Bavaria and Württemberg to become independent kingdoms.

For the Third Coalition, the only significant triumph came at sea where the British under Nelson inflicted a major defeat upon the French and Spanish fleets under Villeneuve at Trafalgar on 21 October 1805. Although Nelson was killed in the engagement, the victory ensured the Royal Navy's mastery of the high seas and effectively ensured that the threat of an invasion of Britain was removed. The most significant lesson learned was that while Britain could ensure the French were defeated at sea; on land, the French continued to reign supreme. The French power was emphasized earlier in the year when, on 26 May, Napoleon was crowned King of Italy in Milan cathedral.

Britain Alone

With the collapse of Austria, the Third Coalition unraveled. The British position was further weakened when, on 15 February 1806, the French and Prussians agreed a treaty under which Prussian ports were closed to British ships. On the same day French troops entered Naples and, on 30 March, Napoleon's brother Joseph became King of Naples. Another of Napoleon's brothers, Louis, became King of the Netherlands on 5 June 1806.

As a result of the Prussian occupation of Hanover, Britain declared war on Prussia on 1 April 1806 and, three days later, renewed its blockade of the French coast. Although the British, under John Stuart, achieved a minor victory at Maida, in southern Italy, on 4 June, this was a temporary success and Stuart retreated back to Sicily. Further north, however, the position continued to deteriorate for the British, with the creation of the Confederation of the Rhine, on 12 July. This body, incorporating *inter alia* Bavaria, Württemberg, Mainz, and Baden, was French dominated, adopting the Napoleonic Code and agreeing to supply troops to the French army. Following its military defeat, Saxony was to join the Confederation, as a result of the Treaty of Posen, on 10 December 1806. However, all was not well in the Franco-Prussian alliance. The latter mistrusted France, believing that Napoleon intended to cede Hanover to Britain as part of a comprehensive peace treaty. Having received an ultimatum from the Prussians, on 1 October, the French emperor responded by marching from Bavaria to threaten Prussia and, on 9 October, Prussia declared war on France. Napoleon defeated the Prussians under Hohenlohe at the Battle of Jena on 14 October. At the same time, another French army, under Louis Davout, defeated a Saxon army under the Duke of Brunswick at Auerstadt. On 27 October the French captured Berlin, the Prussian capital. This success was followed on 7 November with the surrender of the Baltic port of Lübeck, held by Gebhard von Blücher, to the French. French control of the major Prussian strategic cities, such as Spandau and Magdeburg, was quickly achieved and, on 21 November, Napoleon issued his Berlin Decrees. Initiating the "Continental System", these decrees barred all British ships from European ports and declared a blockade of Britain. In response, Britain declared its own blockade of pro-French ports on 7 January 1807; this was further extended on 11 November. Napoleon responded with a tightening of his Continental System, on 17 December 1807, when he issued the Milan Decrees.

The military position continued to deteriorate for the Prussians. On 28 November, the French army, under Joachim Murat, entered Warsaw in its pursuit of the retreating Prussian and Russian armies and Napoleon continued the march eastward into December. However, despite defeating a Russian force at Pultusk on 26 December, the French under Jean Lannes were unable to prevent a further retreat by the Russians. With the winter setting in, both sides ceased offensive actions.

War in the east resumed early in 1807 with the Battle of Eylau on 8 February. The result of the engagement was indecisive, although both sides sustained heavy casualties. Further success, however, followed in March and April with the capture of Danzig. In response to the continuing French successes, Prussia and Russia signed the Convention of Bartenstein on 26 April; Britain joined the Convention two months later on 27 June. However, by that date, the Convention forces had suffered a major defeat at the Battle of Friedland, on 14 June, at the hands of the French commander Lannes. Following this defeat, Russia came to terms with France through the Treaty of Tilsit, signed on 7 July. By this treaty, Russia agreed to the creation of a French client state, the

Gebhard Leberecht von Blücher, Prince of Wahlstadt (1742–1819). After an early career that included being discharged from the army for insubordination, he became "Marshal Forward" and a great commander of men.

Grand Duchy of Warsaw (established formally on 19 July with the pro-French Frederick Augustus, King of Saxony, as its ruler), as well as acknowledging the German Confederation. Russia also agreed to bar British ships from its ports and to endeavor to persuade Denmark, Portugal, and Sweden to join the campaign against Britain. The formal peace treaty with Russia was signed on 20 July, although in late August Tsar Alexander I of Russia refused to ratify it. Despite this refusal, Russia broke off all contact with Britain in late November 1807.

On 9 July, a second Treaty of Tilsit with Prussia, resulted in Prussia losing half its territory, part formed the Grand Duchy of Warsaw while the part west of the Elbe transferred to French control. Prussia also

agreed, like Russia, to enforce the Continental System against British shipping. The ex-Prussian territory to the west of the Elbe was created into the new kingdom of Westphalia with another of Napoleon's brothers, Jérome, as its monarch.

Britain responded to the new European order by again sending its fleet to the Baltic. Fearful that the Danish navy would be turned against it, the Royal Navy attacked Copenhagen during early September. As a result, the Danish fleet surrendered on 7 September, although Denmark remained hostile, officially allying itself to France on 29 October 1807. Also on 7 September, Napoleon's grip on Germany was further extended when Sweden, under its king Gustavus IV Adolphus, ceded control of its province of Pomerania to the French.

The British were even more isolated in southern Europe when, on 27 October, the French and Spanish signed the Treaty of Fontainebleau, by which they agreed to invade Portugal to prevent British use of Portuguese ports. The Peninsular War started on 19 November with French forces invading Portugal and, 10 days later, the Portuguese royal family was evacuated to Brazil under the protection of a Royal Navy force under Sidney Smith. Britain's only consolation was that the Portuguese fleet sailed with its monarch rather than passing into the hands of the French.

By the end of 1807 Britain was effectively isolated in its war against Napoleon. The other main European powers—Austria, Prussia, and Russia—had all been soundly defeated and were, to all intents and purposes, now hostile (Austria, for example, joined the Continental System on 28 February 1808), while many of the smaller nations were actively pro-French.

Wellington — Napoleon's Nemesis

Born in Dublin in 1769 as a younger son of a member of the Anglo-Irish aristocracy, the 1st Earl of Mornington, Arthur Wesley, as he was known, was to join the army in 1787 as an infantry officer. Serving in Ireland, he was promoted and also acted as an MP in the Irish parliament for the constituency of Trim from 1790 until 1795. His first experience of fighting the French came in 1794 when his regiment served in The

Netherlands. His rise to prominence started in 1797 when he was sent to India. His older brother Richard followed him to the sub-continent, being appointed Governor-General the following year.

In India, Arthur Wesley changed his surname to Wellesley and in 1799 he was to bring the British considerable success, being involved in the campaigns against Tipu Sultan in Mysore and Seringapatam. His capable administration of the latter, after its capture, set a standard that he'd go on to match elsewhere. His final triumphs in India were the capture of Poona in 1803 and the victory at Arguam. In 1805 he returned to Britain, being knighted for his success. He married in 1805 and, between 1806 and 1809 served as MP for Rye. Despite his parliamentary role, he also assisted in the British campaign against Denmark in 1807 and was sent, in 1808, to the Iberian Peninsula to assist the Portuguese. He was appointed commander of British forces in the Peninsular War in 1809 and was promoted to a Viscount in July of the same year. His forces eventually swept Napoleon's army out of Spain and, following the defeat of Napoleon and the first Treaty of Paris in 1814, he was created the 1st Duke of Wellington.

On Napoleon's escape from Elba, he took command of a scratch army and, with the aid of Blücher, inflicted the final defeat of Napoleon at Waterloo in 1815. After his military career, Wellington became a prominent figure in British domestic politics, including acting as Prime Minister between 1828 and 1830, and again briefly in 1834. Wellington died in 1852 and was buried in St Paul's Cathedral.

The Peninsular War

On 16 February 1808 French troops in Spain started to take offensive action against their erstwhile allies, capturing Barcelona 13 days later. This policy was part of Napoleon's grand scheme to ensure French domination of the Mediterranean countries. Four days later, on 3 March, Madrid was captured by a French force under Joachim Murat.

However, the reaction of the Spanish to the apparent reversal of their relationship to the French was swift. The Madrid crowd forced the pro-French chief minister, Manuel de Godoy, to resign on 18 March

Map illustrative of
THE MILITARY MOVEMENTS IN
INDIA
from 1797 to 1805,
referred to in the Life of
FIELDMARSHAL THE DUKE OF
WELLINGTON.

By A. Petermann, F.R.G.S.

Scale of English Miles.

and, the following day, the Spanish king, Charles IV, was forced to abdicate, again because of his perceived pro-French bias. He was succeeded by his son Ferdinand; however, Napoleon refused to accept this settlement, forcing both Charles and Ferdinand to renounce their claims to the throne on 6 May 1808. By this date, rebellion had started in Madrid; the rebellion—the 'Dos Mayo'—commenced on 2 May 1808 and was to be marked by guerrilla activity that characterized much of the anti-French activity during this phase of the war.

With the removal of the existing monarch and heir, Napoleon's brother Joseph became King of Spain on 15 June 1808; he was succeeded as King of Naples by Joachim Murat. However, the French were not universally successful in Spain; the first siege of Saragossa lasted between 15 June and 15 August, with the Spanish defenders ensuring that the French were unable to reopen the route from the border through central Spain. More significantly, on 19 July 1808, a French army under Pierre Dupont was heavily defeated at the Battle of Baylen and, on 1 August, a British army, led by Arthur Wellesley (who had recently returned from India), landed in Portugal with the intention of backing the anti-French forces. Moreover, the French puppet king, Joseph, fearful of his position in Madrid, fled the city on 1 August.

Wellesley achieved an almost immediate success with victory over the French at the Battle of Vimeiro on 21 August. This victory resulted, nine days later, in the Convention of Cintra between the British commander Hew Dalrymple and his French counterpart Andoche Junot, for the French evacuation of Portugal. With the military position deteriorating, Napoleon took personal charge of the French forces in Spain in the autumn and, under his command, France retook Madrid on 13 December 1808. This was followed on 16 December by a victory at the Battle of Cardadeu by a French army under Gouvion St-Cyr; St-Cyr had a further success, eight days later, when he defeated another Spanish army, under Aloys Reding, at Molins de Rey. A further indication of the improved French position came with the second siege of Saragossa,

India, 1797–1805. Wellesley made his name in India and helped Britain extend its rule over the subcontinent.

between 20 December 1808 and 20 February 1809, when the Spanish army failed to break the French lines of communication.

Following an agreement of 1 January 1809, Britain and Spain confirmed that neither would seek a separate peace with France. Five days later, on 6 January, the British commander in Spain, Sir John Moore, was killed at the Battle of Coruña. A further setback to anti-French forces occurred on 25 February when St-Cyr defeated Reding again, this time at the Battle of Valls. On 22 April Arthur Wellesley arrived at Lisbon to take command, following the death of Sir John Moore. His impact was immediate, with victory over the French led by Nicholas-Jean Soult at Oporto on 12 May. This defeat forced the French to withdraw from Portugal. A further victory, at the Battle of Talavera, followed on 28 July, forcing the French to retreat toward Madrid. Later that year, however, the French position was partially restored by victory over the Spanish at Ocana and by occupation of Andalusia, with the exception of Cadiz (the capital of free Spain), which was besieged from early 1810 for some 10 months.

On 10 July 1810 Ney captured the town of Ciudad Rodrigo, situated on the border between Spain and Portugal, as a prelude to a further French invasion of Portugal. However, the French were held by the British and Portuguese armies, commanded by Viscount Wellington (as Wellesley had become in late 1809), at Torres Vadras in October 1810; running short of supplies the French were forced to retreat. Elsewhere, Spanish control over its South American empire—in Venezuela, Mexico and Chile, for example—was being eroded as nationalist spirit increased and sentiment against Joseph Bonaparte increased in favor of the overthrown Ferdinand VII.

Following the French defeat at the Battle of Fuentes d'Onoro on 6 May 1811 by Wellington, Napoleon replaced André Massena as commander by Auguste Marmont. However, the French suffered a further setback on 16 May when the British, under William Beresford, defeated a French force, under Soult, at Albuera as the French sought to advance toward Portugal.

On 19 January 1812 the British captured the border town of Ciudad Rodrigo. This town sat astride one of the main routes between Spain and Portugal and control of it helped to secure Portugal. This success was followed, on 6 April, by the capture of Badajoz, a city on the

Michel Ney (1769–1815) commanded Napoleon's rearguard during the retreat from Moscow and was executed by firing squad for treason after Napoleon's fall.

Spanish-Portuguese border and, on 22 July 1812, by a crucial victory over Marmont at Salamanca—after which British forces were able to advance into Spain. The war was now moving inexorably in Wellington's favor. On 12 August, following Joseph Bonaparte's retreat, British forces entered Madrid. However, there were still occasional setbacks: on 19 September, for example, Marmont forced the British to evacuate the city of Burgos.

The Peninsular War came to an end in 1813 with two important British victories. On 21 June Wellington defeated the French under Jean-Baptiste Jourdan at Vittoria, forcing the French to evacuate Spain. Following an attempt by Soult to re-enter Spain, the French were heavily defeated in the Battle of Sorauren at the end of July. Remaining French pockets of resistance in Iberia were gradually eliminated; San Sebastian, for example, surrendered to Wellington after a 10-day siege on 9 September 1813 and Pamplona fell on 31 October. Following his successes in Spain and Portugal, Wellington's army crossed the Spanish-French border on 5 October. The balance of war was now heavily in Wellington's favor. He defeated Soult at Toulouse on 10 November and advanced further into France, laying siege to Bayonne in early December.

From 1808 beyond the Iberian Peninsula

Although the British were primarily concerned with the war against France in Spain, other areas also saw action from 1808 onward. On 2 February 1808 French influence in Italy was further extended by the occupation of Rome by an army led by Sextius Miollis, as a result of Pope Pius VII's refusal to accept the new Kingdom of Naples and the Confederation of the Rhine.

Although Austria, Prussia, and Russia remained non-combatants at this stage, there was unease in all three countries. In early June 1808 the Austrians increased their military capabilities by creating a militia of all males aged between 19 and 25 not already in the army. While, during the same month, the Russians liberalized the position in Finland—a country seized earlier from Sweden—in order to ensure Finnish support in the event of further war. (Russia's control of Finland was

One of the reasons for Wellington's successes in the Peninsular War was his skill in intercepting French messages and cracking their codes. The man behind this was George Scovell (1775–1861), some of whose notes are seen here.

finally conceded by Sweden with the Peace of Frederickshaven, signed on 17 September 1809.) Napoleon's position, however, remained secure, evinced by the fact that he was able to impose a strict limit on the size of the Prussian army in early September. His position was also confirmed through a meeting between the emperor and his Russian counterpart, Alexander I, at Erfurt (a Prussian city under French rule), which reaffirmed earlier agreements between France and Russia over the Balkans and, also, stated that Russia would support France in the event of Austrian aggression.

Under Heinrich von Stein, the Prussian government introduced a number of reforms which the French construed as being hostile; as a result Napoleon declared him an "Enemy of France", forcing him into hiding. However, the reforms undertaken by von Stein were crucial in the reestablishment of Prussia as a serious military force. A further reform, on 1 March 1809, saw the creation of a Prussian General Staff under Gerhard von Scharnhorst.

In early 1809, Francis I of Austria determined that, faced with the threat from France, Austria would re-enter the war. In furtherance of this, on 4 April 1809, the British agreed to provide a subsidy to Austria of £150,000 per month and also invade the Kingdom of Holland. The Austrian army marched through Bavaria, but was defeated at the Battle of Abensberg, on 19/20 March, by Napoleon. Archduke Charles suffered a second defeat at the Battle of Eckmühl on 22 March. Elsewhere, however, Austrian forces, led by Archduke Ferdinand, captured Warsaw—capital of the French-controlled Duchy of Warsaw.

On 13 May the Austrian capital, Vienna, fell to the French and, four days later, Napoleon issued a decree formally annexing the Papal States, which had been occupied by France since February 1808. Not all went Napoleon's way, however, as, after his defeat by the Austrians at the Battle of Aspern-Essling on 21/22 May, the French were forced to retreat. Following the defeat, France requested support from its (lukewarm) ally Russia; limited assistance, however, was provided—except in the north, where a Russian-backed army forced the Austrians to abandon Warsaw on 3 June. Napoleon's fortunes changed with a further victory over Charles at the Battle of Wagram on 5/6 July and by the French capture of Pope Pius VII on 6 July. Austria sued for peace and, on 12 July, an armistice was agreed; this was followed on 14 October by the Peace of Schönbrunn, by which Austria ceded the Illyrian provinces to France and made other territorial concessions.

In the period between the armistice and treaty, Britain fulfilled its pledge to invade the Low Countries with a landing on 28 July. However, it was ill-planned and too late to make an impact. As a result, the British force was quickly withdrawn.

By the Treaty of Paris, signed on 6 January 1810, Sweden joined the Continental System in return for the province of Pomerania. Following the Treaty of Schönbrunn, 1810 was a year of relative peace in mainland Europe. There were some developments, notably the abdication of Louis Bonaparte as King of Holland in early July. Toward the end of the year there was also the annexation, by France, of the ports of Bremen, Hamburg, Hanover, Lauenburg, and Lübeck, as a means of further enforcing the Continental System. It was the French annexation of a further port, Oldenburg, on 22 January 1811, that marked a deterioration in relations between France and Russia.

The March into Russia

Although France and Russia were nominally at peace, a number of events emphasized that there was growing hostility between the two countries. In January 1812 France reoccupied Pomerania in order to persuade Sweden to cease breaking the Continental System and to encourage it not to enter into an alliance with Russia against France. This was followed, on 24 February, by an agreement with Prussia by which French troops were permitted to pass through Prussian territory if necessary. The agreement also allowed for Prussian troops to be provided in any conflict against Russia. The following month saw Austria, worried by the Russian expansion in the Balkans at the expense of the Ottoman empire, also promising to provide troops. In return, Napoleon guaranteed the Ottoman empire and agreed to return the Illyrian provinces to Austria. On 29 March 1812, the pro-French Count Mikhail Speransky was replaced as Secretary of the Council of State by Tsar Alexander I.

Despite French endeavors, Sweden signed the Treaty of Abo with Russia on 9 April, in which Sweden agreed to provide a military diversion in northern Germany to assist Russia in exchange for Russian support for the annexation of Norway from Denmark. A further piece of Alexander's jigsaw fell into place on 28 May 1812 when, by the Treaty of Bucharest, peace was secured with the Ottoman empire.

However, it was to be Napoleon that took the first military action when, on 24 June, the Grande Armée of 100,000 cavalry and 500,000 infantry crossed the River Niemen and invaded Russia. Four days later, the French crossed the River Vilna and captured Vilnius. With Russia and Sweden now at war with France, Britain signed the Treaty of Örebro, on 18 July, agreeing an alliance with them. The French position was also weakened by the fact that, being unwilling to sacrifice Austrian and Prussian support, Napoleon was unable to support the Polish declaration of independence (which had been made on 26 June) and thus sacrificed the potentially significant support of the Poles.

The war continued to Napoleon's advantage with victories over Michel Andreas Barclay de Tolly at Smolensk, on 17/18 August, and over Mikhail Ilarionovich Kutuzov at the Battle of Borodino, on 7 September. The Russian capital, Moscow, was occupied a week later but Napoleon had committed the serious tactical mistake of not deploying his reserves to destroy the remnants of the Russian army. From this point, the war against Russia turned against him.

With winter setting in, the French position deteriorated. Part of the French army under Joachim Murat was defeated at the Battle of Vinkaro on 18 October and, less than a week later, French forces started to withdraw from Moscow. Following defeat at the hands of Kutuzov, at the Battle of Maloytaroslavets on 24 October, Napoleon's preferred route of withdrawal was blocked, thus forcing the army to adopt a longer, more difficult, route. A further major defeat occurred on 26-28 November when the combined Russian army, under Kutuzov and Ludwig Adolf Wittgenstein, inflicted heavy casualties on the French as Napoleon's army sought to cross the River Beresina.

Napoleon's Russian adventure ended in ignominious withdrawal, compounded by the fact that Napoleon himself was forced to leave the army on 5 December and return quickly to Paris in order to regain control after hearing of a failed coup attempt led by Claude-François de Malet. The remnants of the Grande Armée, all 10,000 of them, returned

heavily defeated under the command of Murat later in December. By that date, the French position had been further weakened by the decision of the Prussian commander within the Grande Armée, Yorck von Wartenburg, to break with France.

Napoleon's Defeat

With the defeat of the Grande Armée the period of French domination in Europe was to come quickly to an end. The eventual formation of the Sixth Coalition brought together Austria, Britain, Prussia, and Russia from the early part of 1813 onward, and other countries also joined the anti-French alliance. On 3 March 1813, through the Treaty of Stockholm, Britain agreed to subsidize Sweden to enable the latter to provide an army of 30,000. On 17 March, Prussia declared war on France and, on the following day, Russian troops captured Hamburg. Ten days later, on 28 March, a combined Prussian and Russian force captured Dresden, forcing the puppet king of Saxony, Frederick Augustus, to flee.

On 2 May Napoleon's army defeated a combined Prussian and Russian force at Lützen and a further engagement, at Bautzen, followed on 20/21 May; this battle was, however, indecisive, although leading to heavy casualties on both sides. During the summer there were moves toward a peace treaty, culminating in the Congress of Prague, held between 28 July and 10 August, but it failed to reach a settlement. With the failure of the talks in Prague, Austria formally declared war on 12 August 1813. On 23 August, the French, under Nicolas-Charles Oudinot, were defeated by the Prussians, under Friedrich von Bülow, at Gross-Beeren. Three days later the French, commanded by Jacques MacDonald, were defeated at Katzbach by the Prussians under Gebhard von Blücher. Simultaneously, however, at the Battle of Dresden, Napoleon, who had just arrived, defeated an Austrian army. In early September, the French position in Germany deteriorated further with the Swedish victory at Dennwitz, as Jean-Baptiste Bernadotte's army defeated that of Ney.

The erosion of French support continued in October 1813 when Bavaria left the Confederation of the Rhine and declared war against

France. Napoleon himself was to suffer defeat when, on 16-19 October, his army was crushed at Leipzig—in the "Battle of the Nations", by the combined armies of Austria, Prussia, and Russia—and was forced to retreat. Napoleon's defeat here effectively ended his hopes in Germany, with the collapse of the Confederation of the Rhine and of the Kingdom of Westphalia. In Italy, too, Napoleon's grasp on power was collapsing; on 26 October, the Austrians defeated the French under Eugène de Beauharnais at Valsarno.

Reflecting the changed military balance, in early November the coalition offered France peace terms by which France would have retained some of its military conquests. However, Napoleon failed to respond and, on 1 December, the coalition confirmed its intention to invade France. By that date the French had been forced to leave the Netherlands, on 15-17 November, as a result of Dutch uprisings. The threat to France became all the more apparent when, on 21 December, the Austrians, under Karl Philipp zu Schwarzenburg, invaded from Switzerland and, on 31 December, when the Prussians, under Blücher, crossed the Rhine at Mannheim.

With the collapsing strategic position for France, Napoleon's erstwhile allies sought to safeguard their own position. On 11 January, Joachim Murat, the King of Naples, broke with Napoleon in the hope of retaining his throne. The war was now concentrated on French territory. On 30 January 1814, Napoleon was defeated at the Battle of La Rothière by the combined forces of Austria, Prussia and Russia. Subsequently, the coalition offered Napoleon peace terms, which were rebutted. Napoleon's response came on the battlefield, where he achieved a limited victory at Montereau on 8 February over the Austrians, but the latter were to gain revenge at Bar-sur-Aube on 27 February. Napoleon, continued to fight, gaining victory over Blücher's Prussian army at Craonne on 7 March, However, following the defeat, Blücher combined with the Swedish army under Bernadotte. The French suffered further defeats at Laon, on 9/10 March, at Arcis-sur-Aube, on 20 March, and to the east of Paris, on 30 March.

While the Coalition forces were occupying much of Napoleon's army in the north and east, Wellington was consolidating his position to the south and west. On 12 March, he captured Bordeaux and, on 10 April, defeated a French army under Soult at Toulouse.

By this date, however, Napoleon's reign was at an end. Following the defeat on 30 March, Marmont had surrendered Paris to the coalition on 31 March, with Napoleon, side-tracked to the east of the capital, incapable of coming to its rescue. On the same day the senate declared that the throne was forfeit. On 1 April, coalition troops entered Paris and, on 11 April 1814, Napoleon formally abdicated as a result of the Treaty of Fontainebleau. Napoleon agreed to exile on Elba and, with his departure, the way was open to the new French king, Louis XVIII, to take the throne. A comprehensive peace settlement, the Congress of Vienna, was constituted from 1 November 1814.

War in the Colonies

The French Revolutionary and Napoleonic Wars were marked by the continued efforts of both nations to extend influence outside Europe. Although, for the French, this policy was complicated by a belief in extending the tenets of the revolution to its overseas colonies, initially in terms of allowing self-government and of the abolition of slavery (on 4 February 1794).

One of Britain's first steps after the declaration of war was to act against the remaining French possessions in India. In 1794, British naval forces captured the French territory of the Seychelles in the Indian Ocean and the islands of Guadeloupe, Martinique, and St Lucia in the West Indies, although French forces soon recaptured Guadeloupe and, in June 1795, St Lucia.

Following the French assault on the Dutch Republic, the Dutch colony of Ceylon was surrendered to the British in February 1795; this was followed by a further British territorial gain at the expense of the Dutch when, in September of the same year, forces under James Craig captured the Cape of Hood Hope on behalf of Prince William V of Orange, who had taken refuge in Britain.

Right: After the battle of Waterloo a medal was issued to those who took part. This unclaimed medal should have gone to Gunner William Gallas.

REGIMENT OF ARTILLERY of the King's German Legion,
whereof Lieut. General Baron DECKEN is Colonel.

These are to certify that *Gunner William Gallas & the 2nd Troop of Horse* in the Regiment of Artillery aforesaid, born *at Rodebach in the County of Pelser* hath served in the said Regiment for the space of *Five* Years *Thirty one* Days as likewise in other Corps, according to the following Statement, but in consequence of the Reduction of the several Corps composing the King's German Legion is hereby discharged; having first received all just demands of .... the entry in the said Regiment to the date of this Discharge.

.... prevent any improper use being made of this Discharge, by its falling into other hands, the following is a Description .... *William Gallas* .... *20* Years of Age, is *5* Feet *6* Inches in Hight, *blue* Eyes *fresh* Complexion. *brown hair*

STATEMENT OF SERVICE.

IN WHAT CORPS	PERIOD		Staff Serj.		Serjeant		Corporal		Bombard.		Gunner		Driver		TOTAL SERVICE.	
		to	Years	Days	Years	Days	Years	Days	Years	Days	Years	Days	Years	Days	Years	Days
Artillery K. G. Legion	*25th January 1813*	*24th February 1816*											*5*	*31*	*5*	*31*
									N.B. including two Years as Waterloo Man							

Given under my hand at HANNOVER this *24th* day of *February* 1816.

A Rottiger
Colonel

As a result of the peace treaty with Spain, on 27 July 1795, France gained control of the western part of the island of San Domingo, a region later known as Haiti. Not all went the French way in the West Indies, however, as, on 14 February, the Royal Navy under John Jervis and Horatio Nelson defeated the French at the Battle of Cape St Vincent on 14 February 1796. One of the great naval victories of the war, the result was that British power increased in the region and, during the year, British forces occupied territories formerly held by the Dutch, Spanish and French (Demerara, Essequibo, Berbice, St Lucia, and Grenada). The British, however, abandoned Corsica to the French. This British loss in the Mediterranean was, eventually, balanced in July by the capture of Elba, off the Italian coast.

In the West Indies, British power was further increased in February 1797 when a force under Ralph Abercromby captured the island of Trinidad. This was followed by the seizure in 1798 of Honduras, in Central America, from the Spaniards. Another territorial acquisition by Britain during 1798 from Spain was the island of Minorca.

In India, British power was also enhanced by taking control of Mysore in 1799 and the defeat of the pro-French Tippu Sultan, the Sultan of Mysore, at the Battle of Seringapatam on 4 May 1799. Mysore was divided between Britain and the pro-British ruler of Hyderabad.

Back in the West Indies, the island of Haiti was recaptured during 1801 by a French force under Charles Leclerc. On 3 March 1801, in response to the creation of the Armed Neutrality of the North, Britain seized islands in the West Indies belonging to Denmark and Sweden (most notably St Croix and St Thomas).

Following the collapse of the Treaty of Amiens in May 1803, Britain occupied the French islands of St Lucia and Tobago in the Caribbean. In India, too, the British continued to take offensive action with one figure, Arthur Wellesley (later the Duke of Wellington), coming increasingly to prominence.

In 1809 Britain captured Cayenne and Martinique from the French and also agreed a treaty with the Sikhs that established the boundaries

Right: A page of Wellington's Waterloo despatch written the night after battle.

of British power in northwest India. In 1810, Britain captured Guadeloupe, the last French possession in the West Indies, as well as Mauritius and Bourbon in the Indian Ocean. In the East Indies, the British seized the Dutch territory of Java as a result of the French absorption of the Netherlands into the Empire.

With the end of the war in 1814/15, many of the colonial possessions reverted to their original owners, although Britain did make considerable territorial gains as a result in India, southern Africa and the West Indies.

Napoleon's Domestic Reforms

Many aspects of French life had been radically altered by the Revolution. Local government had been shaken up through the creation of the Departments, and even areas as fundamental as the names for the months of the year had been changed. Napoleon, too, continued to undertake significant reforms, many of which still underpin French law in the 21st century.

On 21 March 1804 a new Civil Code—renamed the Code Napoleon in 1807—was introduced. For the first time this code brought into being a common civil law throughout France; up until this point northern France had civil law based upon custom, while that in southern France was based on Roman Law.

The role of the church was significantly reduced; on 17 February 1810, for example, the Senate effectively ended the power of the papacy within the Empire, when it decreed that no foreign power could exercise spiritual control within France.

The War of 1812

The war of 1812–14 was arguably one of the most unnecessary in history, but resulted from Britain's naval blockade of France during the Napoleonic Wars affecting American merchant shipping and trade. The US, under President Jefferson, in 1807–9, imposed a trade embargo on Britain. This, however, failed and further deterioration in relations

between the two nations led to the USA declaring war in 1812. Untrained US forces attacked the British in Canada and a series of battles were fought in the area of the Great Lakes; these battles, with neither side achieving dominance, gained neither the US nor the British forces a great advantage. However, toward the end of the war, British forces swept southward from Lake Champlain and captured Washington, destroying the White House in August 1814. However, a British attempt to land forces at New Orleans was soundly defeated by US forces under Andrew Jackson, with hostilities extending for the period from 23 December 1814 to 8 January 1815. This battle was one of the most important fought during the British-US War of 1812-14; ironically, the engagement took place after the Treaty of Ghent (December 1814) had settled the war, but such was the slowness in getting the information to North America that the battle took place.

Napoleon's One Hundred Days

Following the Treaty of Fontainebleau, Napoleon abdicated the throne of France on 11 April 1814 and was banished to the island of Elba, located in the Mediterranean off the west coast of Italy. Although exiled, as part of the settlement, he was granted a pension of two million Francs per annum.

However, this was not to be the last that Europe saw of Napoleon as, on 1 March 1815, having escaped from Elba, the emperor landed at Cannes, on the Mediterranean coast, and marched on Paris. Gauging the popular sympathy for the returning Napoleon, the new French King, Louis XVIII, fled the capital city on 19 March and, on the following day, Napoleon entered Paris in triumph, forming a new government largely comprising ministers who had served him before 1814.

In order to counter the threat from Napoleon, the Seventh Coalition was formed, on 25 March 1815, by Austria, Britain, Prussia, and Russia, with each of the members of the alliance agreeing to supply 150,000 troops to the renewed campaign against France. On 5 April, the Duke of Wellington landed in Belgium, then still French-occupied, to lead the British and Dutch armies against Napoleon. On 10 April, the Austrians declared war against the pro-French King of

Above: Some of the survivors of Waterloo lived into the 20th century. This is Paul Abraham of the 7th Regiment French Infantry.

Naples, Joachim Murat, following his occupation of the cities of Bologna, Florence, and Rome. Murat's forces were to be comprehensively defeated by the Austrians at the Battle of Tolentino on 3 May 1815. Another of the pro-French monarchs, King Frederick Augustus of Saxony, was also marginalized by the signing of a peace treaty with Austria, Prussia and Russia on 18 May 1815.

Domestically, Napoleon sought to stabilize his position by reclaiming his status as a revolutionary. In furtherance of this he issued a highly liberal constitution, "Le Champ de Mai", on 2 June, while claiming that he had acted to safeguard the Republic from the potential excesses of a restored monarchy. While Napoleon was occupied in France, the other European powers agreed, on 9 June, at the conclusion of the Congress of Vienna, the postwar settlement.

Among the agreements at the Congress, a new country, the United Netherlands, was created out of Belgium, the Netherlands, and Luxembourg. Poland was split between Russia and Prussia, with Krakow established as a separate republic. Prussia also gained the Rhineland and North Saxony. Elsewhere in Germany, Hanover, of which King George III of Britain was Elector (i.e. head of state), gained Hildesheim and East Friesland, while the German Confederation, under Austrian control, was also created. Ferdinand IV became King of the Two Sicilies, while the Bourbon monarchy in Spain and the Braganza monarchy in Portugal were also restored. Britain's position was further enhanced by the retention of a number of the overseas territories it had conquered during the war, such as Heligoland (off the German coast, ceded by Denmark) and Malta.

However, this postwar settlement might have come to nothing if Napoleon had been able to recreate the military successes he had achieved earlier. Initially, Napoleon's new military campaign went well, with victory over the German army led by General Gebhard von Blücher at Ligny, in Belgium, on 16 June. This was an attempt to split the British, under Wellington, from their potential allies; in the event, despite his defeat, Blücher was able to retreat northward, rather than eastward, as Napoleon had hoped, and thus link up with Wellington.

The scene was now set for the decisive battle of Napoleon's new campaign—the battle we know as Waterloo—on 18 June. Having forced the British and Dutch forces under Wellington northward,

Napoleon engaged his foe just to the south of Brussels. At first, the advantage seemed to lie with Napoleon, but Wellington's men held firm in the superb defensive position that Wellington had chosen to fight. Whether Napoleon would have been completely defeated without the arrival of "Marshal Forward" is hard to say, but the Allies victory was assured by the timely arrival of the Prussians under Blücher. Although defeated two days earlier, Blücher had managed to evade the harrying French forces of Marshal Emanuel de Grouchy and was thus able to launch an assault on Napoleon's right flank. Sensing that this was the decisive moment of the battle, Wellington launched a counter-attack, forcing the French to retreat.

Four days after his final defeat at Waterloo, Napoleon was to abdicate again, on 22 June. This time there was to be no return; following agreement between Britain, Prussia, Russia, and Austria, it was decided in early August that the ex-emperor would be sent into exile on the remote British colony of St Helena in the mid-Atlantic, where he was to die, aged 52, on 5 May 1821.

Napoleon's death at such a relatively early age has led to claims over the years that he was a victim of a murderous plot and that he was in fact poisoned, possibly by arsenic. However, it is now believed that his death was simply the result of natural causes. After his death, Bonaparte's body was eventually repatriated to France and was placed in a dramatic tomb, designed by Visconti and built between 1843 and 1861, within the crypt of the Dôme des Invalides. The mausoleum also contains the bronze sarcophagus of Napoleon's only legitimate son, Napoleon II (1811–32).

The Legacy

The French Revolutionary and Napoleonic wars represented the last pan-European conflict for almost a century. However, within the structures created by the Congress of Vienna were the seeds that would ultimately result in the destruction of two World Wars in the 20th century. In the Low Countries, the creation of the United Netherlands proved to be shortlived, while the increasing dominance of Prussia in Germany would ultimately lead to the creation of a united Germany.

Elsewhere, increased national awareness would lead to instability in central Europe and the Balkans—instability would result, finally, in an assassin's bullets at Sarajevo in 1914 and the slaughter of millions.

Note on the Maps

Most of the maps illustrated in this book have been drawn from the large collection held by the Public Record Office at Kew in west London. This is the major holding of all public documents in the United Kingdom. The maps are derived from three main government departments—the Foreign Office, the Colonial Office, and the War Office—and reflect the interests and concerns at the time they were compiled. Because this is the main source for this book, it is unsurprising that its collection is strongest on the Peninsular War and other places—Copenhagen, Walcheren, and the naval war—that saw British action. However, although the majority of the maps were produced by English-speaking cartographers, the collection also includes numerous maps produced for other nations involved in the French Revolutionary and Napoleonic Wars. To give this book balance and provide information on Napoleon's great European victories, a number of maps have been sourced from 19th century books, particularly from the Hampden Maps collection.

Coalitions against France

Between 1792 and 1815 there were numerous European alliances and treaties that led to coalitions against France. Today we recognize seven wars by coalitions, and these are mentioned in the text and captions:

Number	Dates	Main countries involved
First	1792–97	At first GB, Prussia, Austria, Spain, Naples; at end GB Austria
Second	1799–1802	GB, Portugal, Russia, Austria, Naples
Third	1805	GB, Sweden, Russia, Austria, Naples
Fourth	1806–07	Prussia, Saxony, Russia
Fifth	1809	GB, Austria
Sixth	1812–1814	Ultimately GB, Prussia, Russia, Austria
Seventh	1815	All

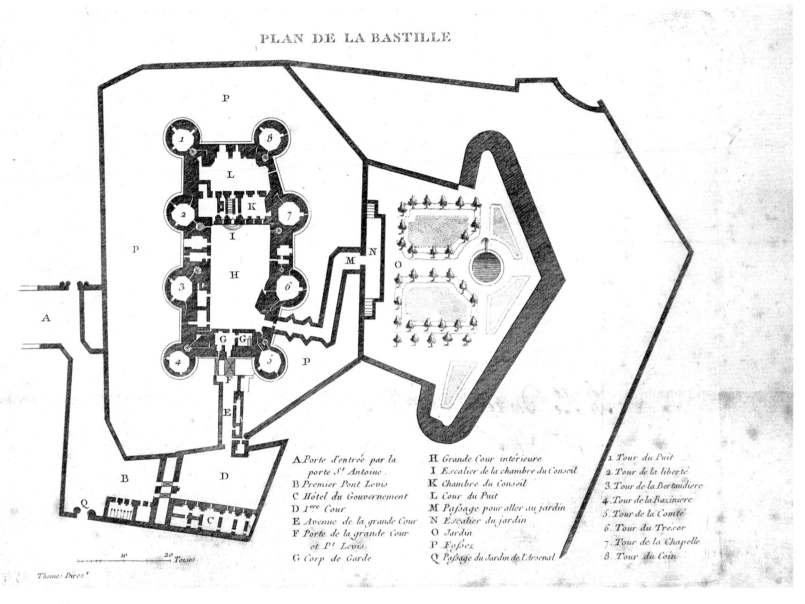

A Porte d'entrée par la
    porte St Antoine.
B Premier Pont Levis
C Hôtel du Gouvernement
D 1ère Cour
E Avenue de la grande Cour
F Porte de la grande Cour
    et Pt Levis
G Corp de Garde

H Grande Cour intérieure
I Escalier de la chambre du Conseil
K Chambre du Conseil
L Cour du Puit
M Passage pour aller au jardin
N Escalier du jardin
O Jardin
P Fossez
Q Passage du Jardin de l'Arsenal

1 Tour du Puit
2 Tour de la liberté
3 Tour de la Bertaudiere
4 Tour de la Baziniere
5 Tour de la Comté
6 Tour du Tresor
7 Tour de la Chapelle
8 Tour du Coin

Thomas Dirext

The Bastille, 1789

On 14 July 1789 a small crowd of civilians along with two detachments of
Gardes françaises and five cannon besieged the royal fortress of the Bastille—
the symbol of despotism. It quickly capitulated and Louis XVI (1754-93) had
effectively lost his capital. In the French provinces the fall of the Bastille
"triggered an orgy of attacks on forty thousand other bastilles." *La Grande
Peur*—the Great Fear—started and the revolution reached critical mass:
nothing would now be able to halt it.

France, 1790

"A correct map of France according to the new divisions into metropolitan circles, departments and districts; as decreed by the National Assembly, January 15, 1790 from a reduced copy of Monsr Cassini's large map with the addition of the adjacent countries from the latest surveys." Beneath the cartouche it is noted, "The two additional departments of Mont Blanc and the Maritim Alps have been decreed since the conquest of Savoy, and the County of Nice." This took place in 1792.

This, then, is the France of the revolution, before Napoleon who was still learning his trade as an artillery officer when this map was drawn up. Compare it to the map of France on page 140 following the second Treaty of Paris (1815) and the Congress of Vienna. There's little difference: after all Napoleon's campaigns, all his soldiers' efforts, and twenty years of warfare the 1790 boundaries of France were those granted to France after Napoleon's fall.

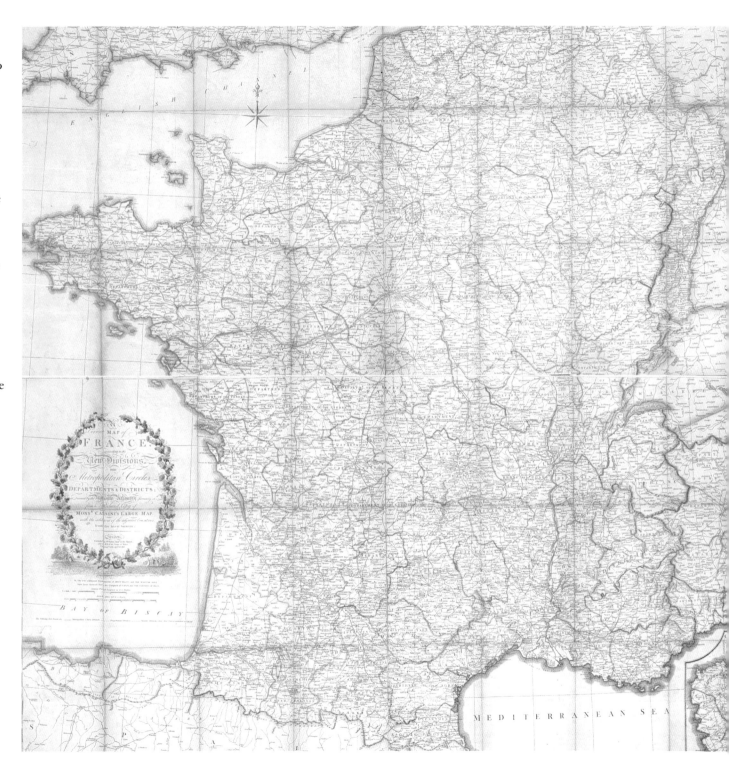

The Glorious First of June, 1794

The first big sea battle of the revolutionary wars took place off the coast of Brittany between the relatively inexperienced French admiral Louis Thomas Villaret de Joyeuse (1748–1812) and the veteran ex-Navy Minister Richard Howe (1726–99). Sent to escort a food convoy from the United States, Villaret's 26 ships met Howe's 25 in a battle that would see nearly 5,000 casualties, 3,500 of them French. More concerned with their six French prizes than the strategically important convoy, the British allowed their victory to become a strategic setback as the blockade was pierced.

The map shows the track of one of the English vessels from 17 May to 1 June 1794.

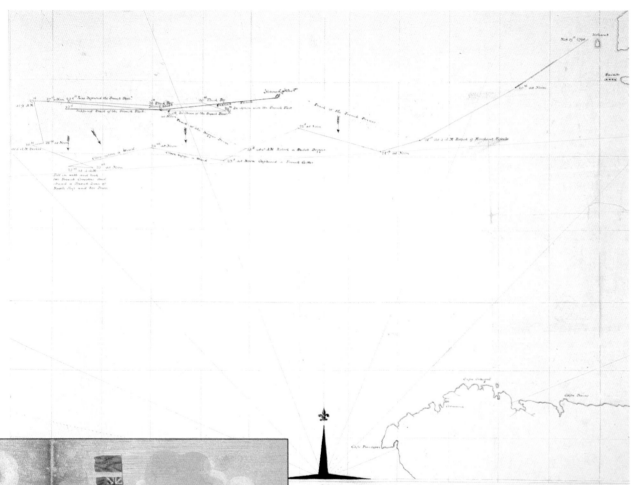

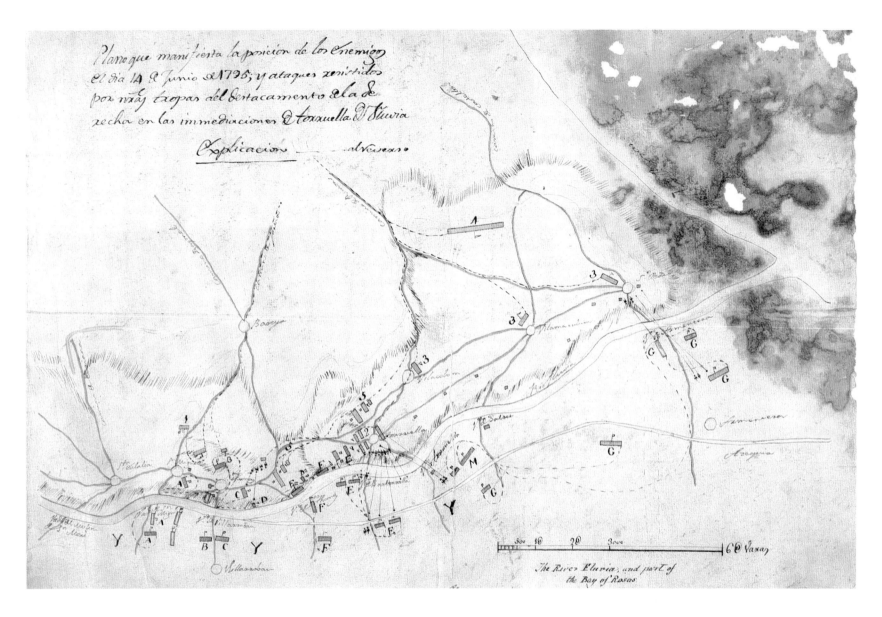

The River Fluvia, and part of
the Bay of Rosas

Battles of the Fluvia, 1795

France went to war with Prussia (and, because of that country's alliance, Austria) in April 1792 and, swiftly, her fractured army was pushed back; Paris was threatened. The French response was dramatic: first the monarch was arrested and the republic declared (Louis XVI would be executed on 21 January 1793); next the enemy was turned back at Valmy on 20 September; Belgium was conquered by General Charles Dumouriez (1739–1823) and Savoy annexed. Defeated at Valmy, the Prussians retreated and were joined in the first anti-French coalition of the period by Britain, Portugal, Spain, the Netherlands, Naples, and others. Total mobilization by the French led to victories by General Jean-Baptiste Jourdan (1762–1833) at Wattignies in 1793 and Fleurus in 1794. General Barthélemy Schérer (1747–1804) attacked the Spanish on the Pyrenean Front in April 1795 along the River Fluvia in Catalonia. Fierce fighting in the area was inconclusive and both sides halted to await the outcome of peace negotiations.

Europe, 1796

"A new map of the Seat of War exhibiting the post roads of Germany, Hungary and the Netherlands and those of the adjacent parts of France, Switzerland, Italy and Poland from the Large Map published in Vienna by the order of Joseph II Emperor of the Romans with several additions." Published by Laurie and Whittle with the dominions of the Holy Roman Emperor colored in yellow. Note at far right Buchovina "New District taken from the Turks." For so long the bogeyman of Europe, the Ottoman Empire's high water mark had been its final attempt on Vienna in 1683. Since that date its conquests had been rolled back and by the end of the 18th century its territories were being eyed up by many of the great European powers.

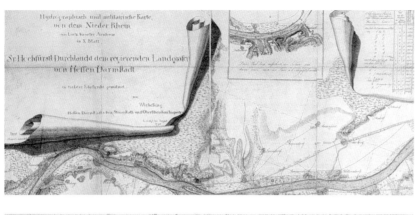

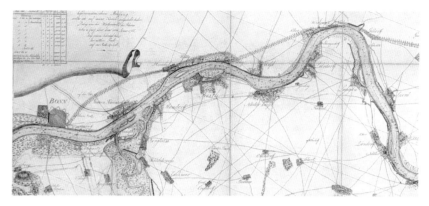

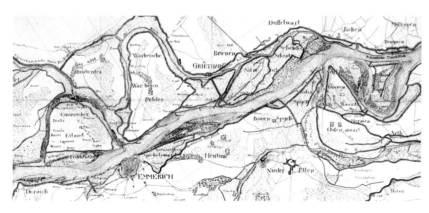

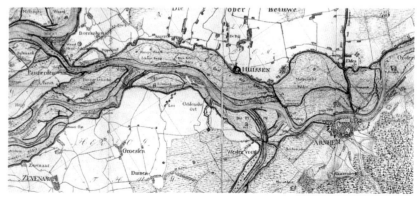

The Rhine, 1796

"Hydrographic and military map of the lower Rhine from Linz to Arnhem." Finished in 1796, although this version was published some years after, this splendid map (not all shown) provides interesting details of the Rhine's fortified towns, such as Cöln (today Köln/Cologne). Students of later periods of history and other conflicts will note Arnhem and Oosterbeck (Bottom Right), Remagen (Center Right) and Bonn (Top Right). In 1795 the treaty of Basle with the

Prussians secured the neutrality of northern Germany until 1806. The Prussians gave up their lands west of the Rhine in return for lands on the east bank and a free hand in Poland, whose lands were partitioned by Prussia, Russia, and Austria three times in the late eighteenth century (see page 141).

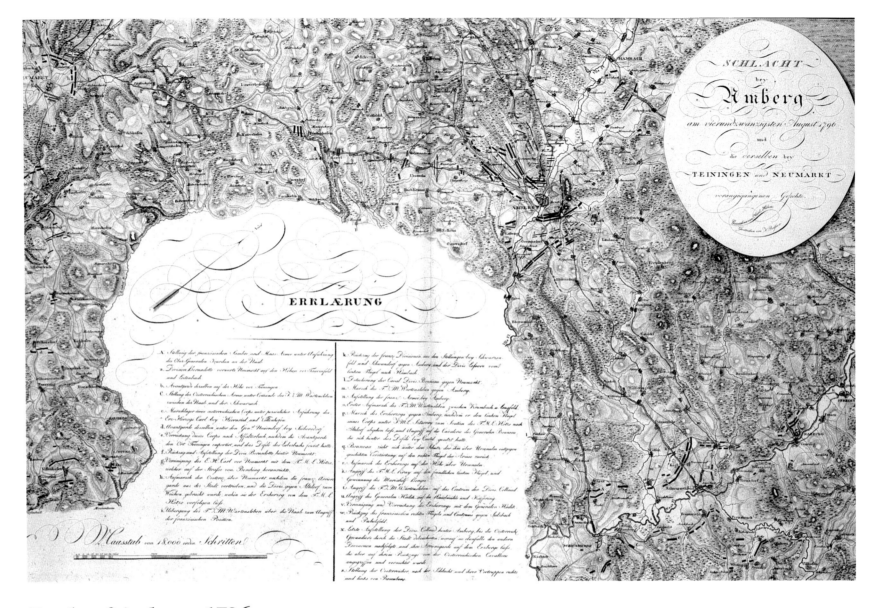

Battle of Amberg, 1796

In 1795 the Franco-Prussian treaty of Basle secured the neutrality of northern Germany until 1806; one with the Spanish (Ildefonso in 1796) saw them join forces with the French. This allowed French troops to advance on various fronts, under General Napoleon in Italy (see pages 40, 41 and 43–47) and under General Jourdan in southern Germany. The French thrust in southern Germany was pushed back by the best Austrian commander of the period, Archduke Charles (1771–1847), younger brother of Habsburg emperor Francis II (1768–1835), at the battles of Amberg on 24 August and Würzburg on 15 September. Wounded at Amberg was the British representative to the Austrian headquarters, Charles Crauford (1761–1821), who had been accompanied by his brother Robert Crauford— 'Black Bob' of Peninsular War fame (see page 97). This German map shows the battles of Teiningen and Neumarkt that led up to the battle of Amberg, as drawn by Oberleutnant Höhm.

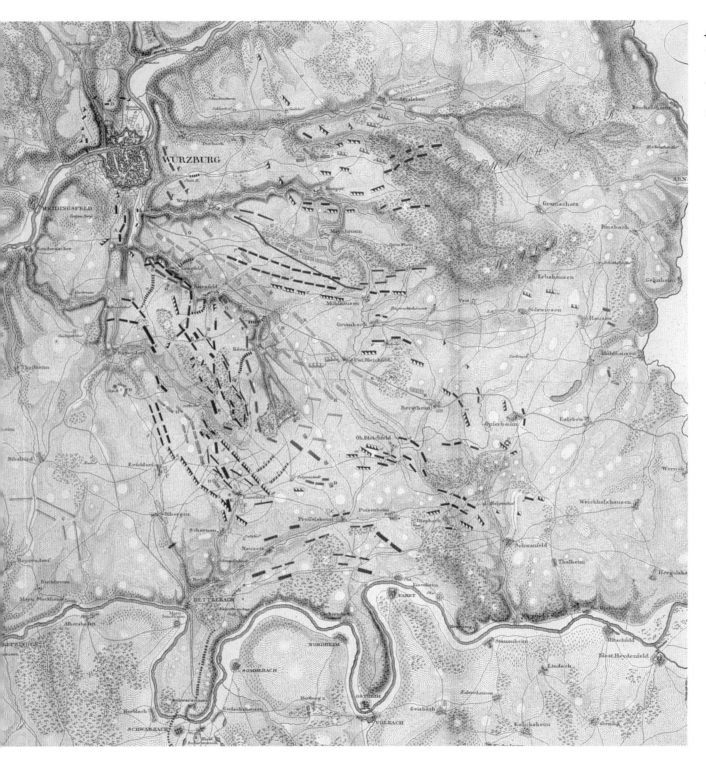

Battle of Würzburg, 1796

The clinching battle in the war of 1792-97, Würzburg saw the Austrians repulse the French.

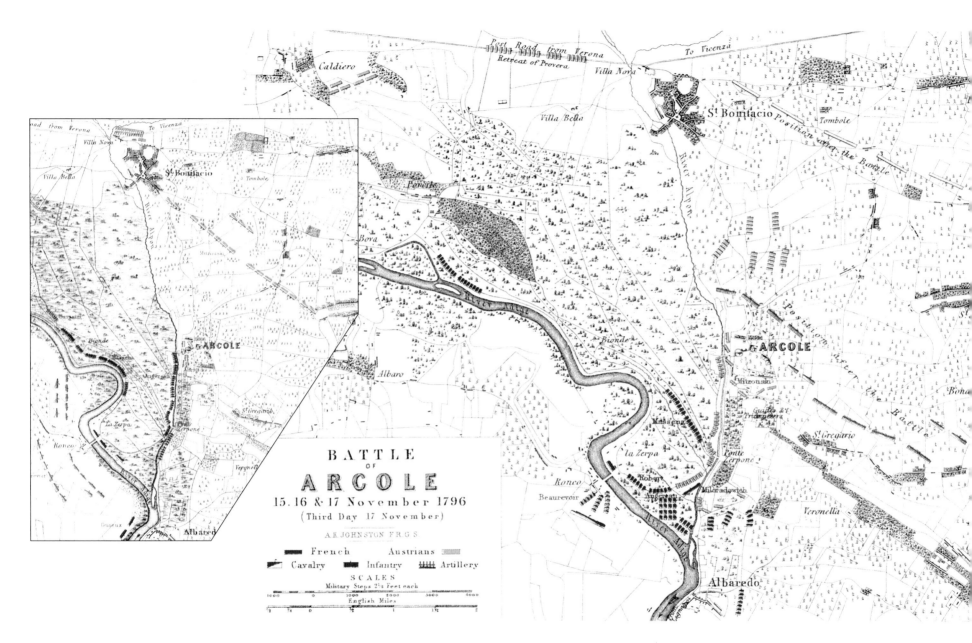

BATTLE
OF
ARCOLE
15. 16 & 17 November 1796
(Third Day 17 November)

A.K. JOHNSTON F.R.G.S.

French   Austrians

Cavalry   Infantry   Artillery

SCALES
Military Steps 2½ Feet each

English Miles

Battle of Arcola, 1796

Unlike their forces in Germany, in Italy the French held the upper hand thanks to the brilliance of their young commander, Napoleon Bonaparte. During the five-year long Italian campaign (1792–97) between France and the first coalition, the Austrians had held the upper hand but after Napoleon took over command of the Army of Italy (he arrived on 27 March 1796) the tables were turned. The young General Bonaparte's tactical acumen was shown in this dazzling and

important victory over larger Austrian forces. Fought between 15 and 17 November around the town of Arcola on the River Alpone, the battle could have gone either way, but the brilliance of Napoleon finally overcame Austrian commander-in-chief Josef d'Alvinitzi (1735–1810). The two maps show [Inset] the first day, the 15th, and the final day, the 17th, and the retreat of the Austrians.

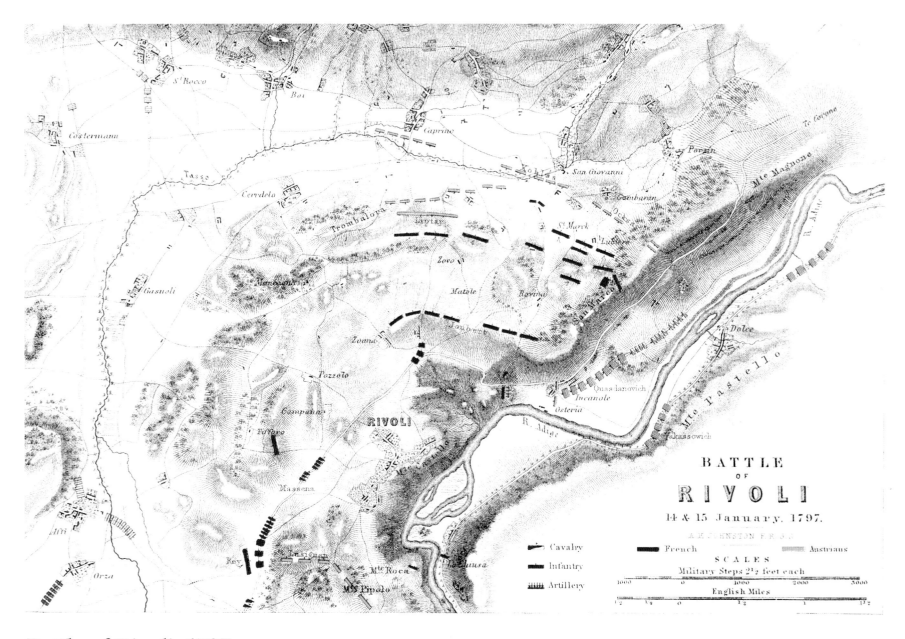

Battle of Rivoli, 1797

The same opponents—Napoleon and d'Alvinitzi—fought again on 14–15 January 1797, as d'Alvinitzi tried to relieve the besieged fortress of Mantua. He failed, suffering some 14,000 dead at this battle. Mantua surrendered on 2 February and after Napoleon had seen off another Austrian attack (by Archduke Charles) a peace treaty was signed that was formalized at Campo Formio on 17 October 1797.

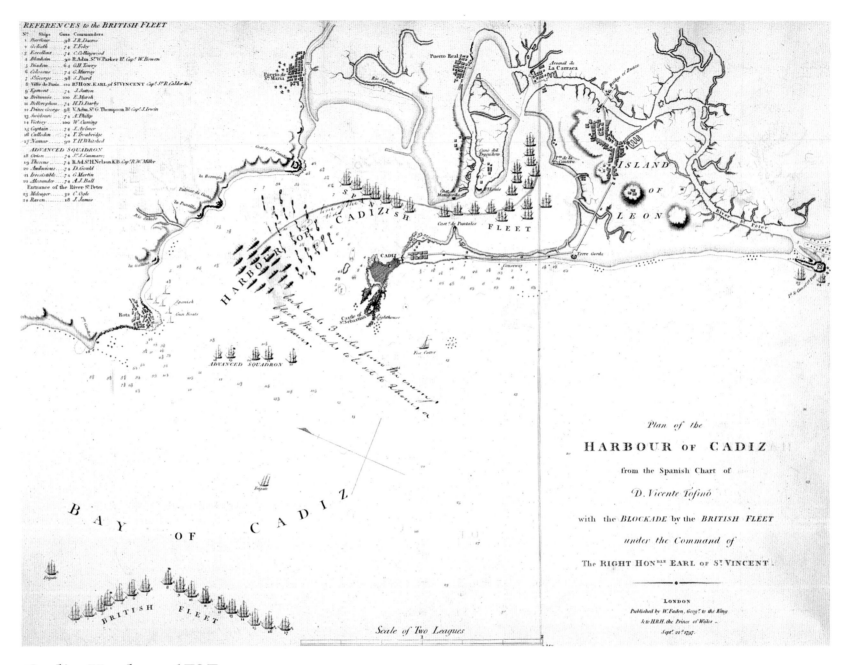

Cadiz Harbor, 1797

"Plan of the harbor of Cadiz from the Spanish chart of D. Vicente Tofino with the blockade of the British fleet under the command of the Right Honourable Earl of St. Vincent". Published in London on 22 September 1797, the key to this map lists the 24 ships of the command of John Jervis, Earl of St. Vincent, blockading the Spanish fleet, including the *Ville de Paris*, his flagship. Until 1796 allied to the British against the French, in 1796 the Spaniards changed sides.

On 14 February 1797 a 27-strong Spanish fleet under Don José de Cordova headed toward Brest to join the French Atlantic squadron. Cordova's fleet was intercepted by Admiral Sir John Jervis's command, that included among its 15 vessels his then flagship, HMS *Victory*, and the *Captain* commanded by Commodore Nelson. The resulting battle saw the Spanish soundly beaten and the remnants blockaded in Cadiz harbor.

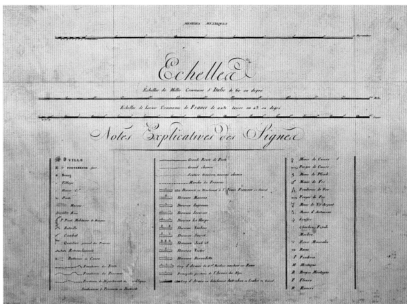

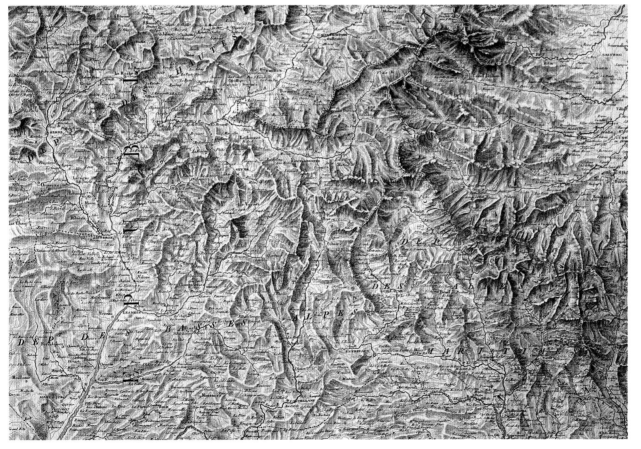

Italy and Southeast Europe, 1792–98

Some sheets of a remarkable 30-sheet map "General map of the theater of war in Italy and in the Alps after the passage of the Var on 29 September 1792 up to the entry of the French into Rome on 22 Pluviose [see note below] in the Republic's sixth year with the limits and divisions of the Republic's new territories by Bacler Dalbe, geographic engineer attached during the whole war to General Napoleon . . ."

Above Left: The cartouche.
Above: Scale and key.
Left: Provence and the Alps.

Note: In 1793 the French produced a new calendar that was backdated to the day the Republic was proclaimed—22 September 1792. While it was officially kept for 14 years (until 1 January 1806), in reality it was used only by the most staunch revolutionaries. *Pluviose* (the month of rains) was the fifth of 12 30-day months of the year.

Golfe de Genes

44

Left: The Italian riviera from Bordighera to Pto Venere.

Right: Corsica, birthplace of Napoleon. Genoese for over 300 years, the island was sold to the French in 1768 and was in rebellion against French rule since that time. Taken by British troops, with Nelson's assistance, in 1794, Napoleon's Italian victories led the British to evacuate the island in 1796, allowing the return of the French.

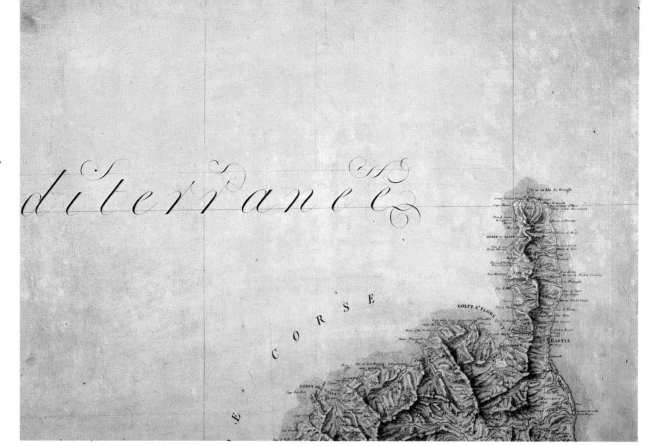

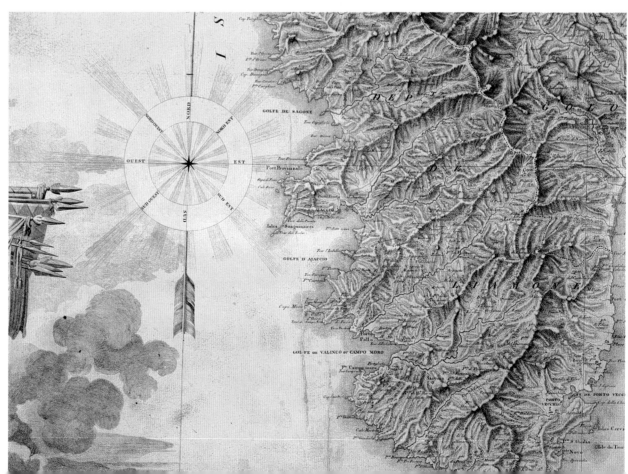

46

Left: The advance on Rome.

Above: "The islands and fortresses hitherto Venetian ceded to the French Republic by the Treaty of Campo Formio [October 1796] on the coast of ancient Greece and Albania. The islands are divided into three Republican departments: the Cyclades (Corfu, Paxos, Antipaxos, etc); Ithaca (Cephalonia, Ithaca, etc); and Aegean (Zante, etc)."

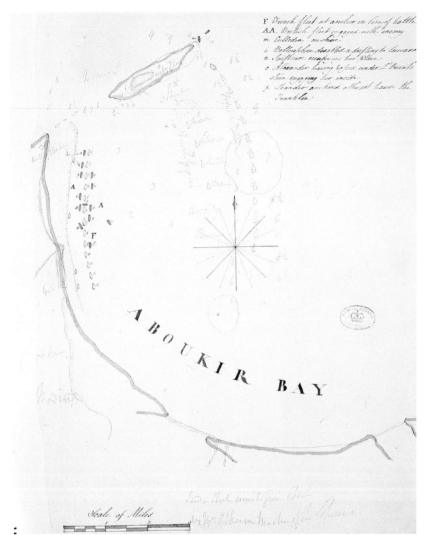

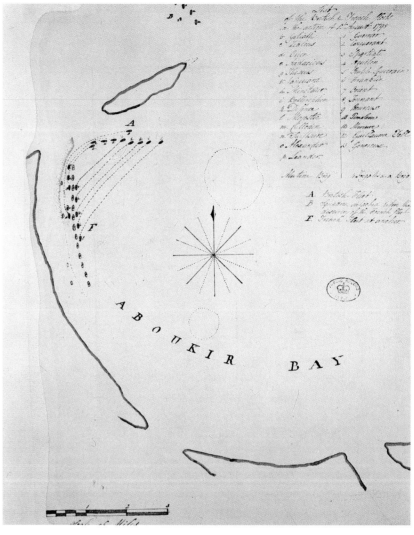

Battle of the Nile, 1798

The first of Nelson's great victories. The first two maps (**Above** and **Above Right**) show the battle and list the fleets:

The British

A British Fleet
B Squadron detached before the
    discovery of the French fleet
F French fleet at anchor
b *Goliath*
c *Zealous*
d *Orion*
e *Audacious*
g *Theseus*
v *Vanguard*
h *Minotaur*
i *Bellerophon*
k *Defense*
l *Majestic*
m *Culloden*
n *Swiftsure*
o *Alexander*
p *Leander*

The French

1 *Guerrier*
2 *Conquerant*
3 *Spartiale*
4 *Aquilon*
5 *Peuple Souverain*
6 *Franklin*
7 *Orient*
8 *Tonnant*
9 *Heureux*
11 *Timoleon*
10 *Mercure*
12 *Guillaume Tell*
13 *Genereux*

Right: "An exact representation of the English and French fleets under the command of Rear-Admiral Sir Horatio Nelson KB and Admiral Brueys off the mouth of the Nile on the 1st of August 1798."

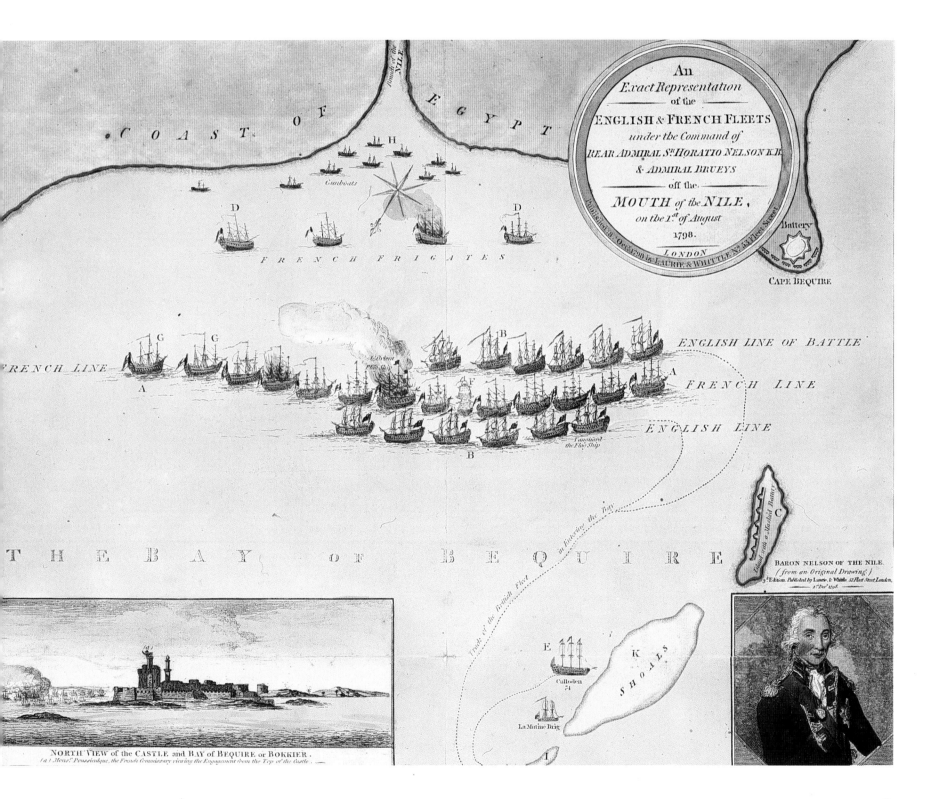

Egypt, 1801

Right: "A Plan of operations of the British forces in Egypt from the landing at Aboukir Bay on the 8th of March to the Battle of Alexandria March 21st inclusive." Lt-Gen Sir Ralph Abercromby KB and some 15,000 troops were sent to Egypt in spring 1801 to stop all possibility of the French securing their position in Egypt. Napoleon had returned to France in August 1800 leaving General Kléber in charge. Following his assassination General Menou took over and it was his forces that were defeated by Abercromby, who died in the battle.

Below Right: Annotated in 1888 by a later British expedition, this map is captioned "The only map of Egypt we had at our landing under command of Sir Ralph Abercromby." It shows the Nile Delta, with Cairo at the bottom and Alexandria at top left.

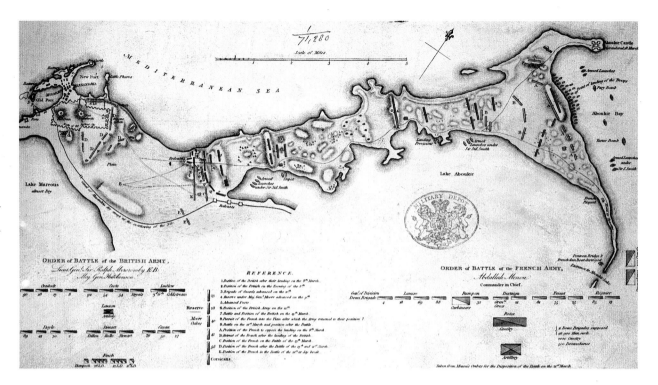

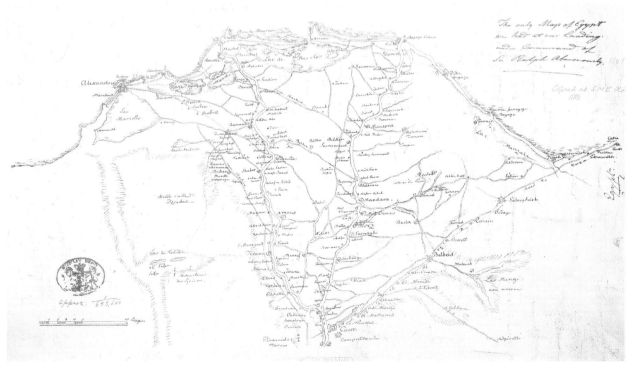

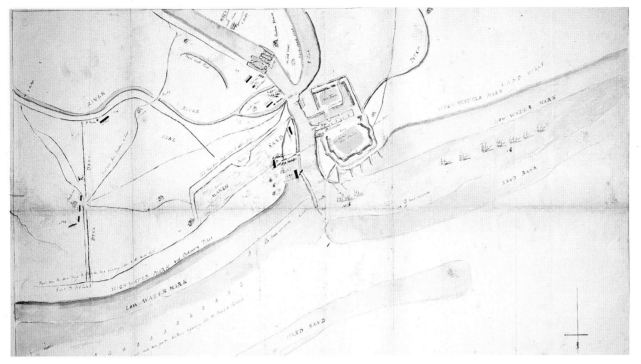

Ostende, 1798

Left: This sketch outlines the plan of the amphibious attack on Ostende by the British in May 1798. The attack was designed to destroy the Ostende-Bruges canal locks, thus depriving the French of a means of concentrating forces for an invasion of England. The Royal Navy force was commanded by Commodore Popham and the 1,200 troops by General Eyre Coote. The force sailed from Margate and reached Ostende without problem. Coote's men destroyed the sluice gates and some small vessels but rising winds meant that Popham couldn't retrieve the landing party. It was forced to surrender to the French garrison the next day.

Courtrai, 1800

Below Left: An important fortified town in Flanders, Courtrai (Kortrijk) shows off the diamond-shaped bastions that dominated military architecture from the 17th century. Belgium's towns and cities needed to be fortified. They had been the cockpit of war for so much of the sixteenth and seventeenth centuries, as they tried to shrug off the Habsburg yoke. The Napoleonic period saw Flanders taken under French rule in a campaign that started in April 1792. In May 1794 troops of the first coalition attempted at Courtrai to stop the French attack on Flanders. It was no good: by 1795 the area was under French control.

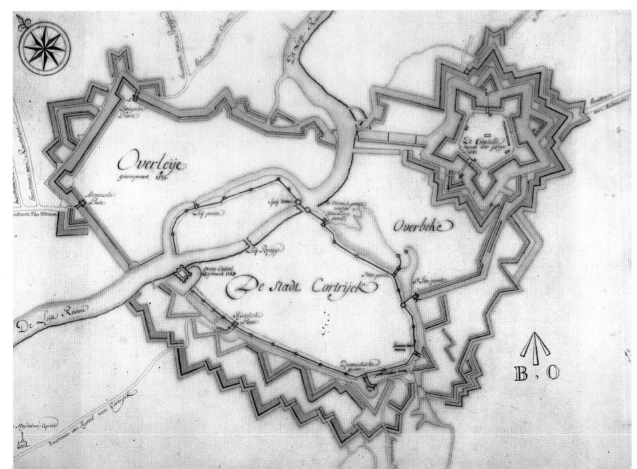

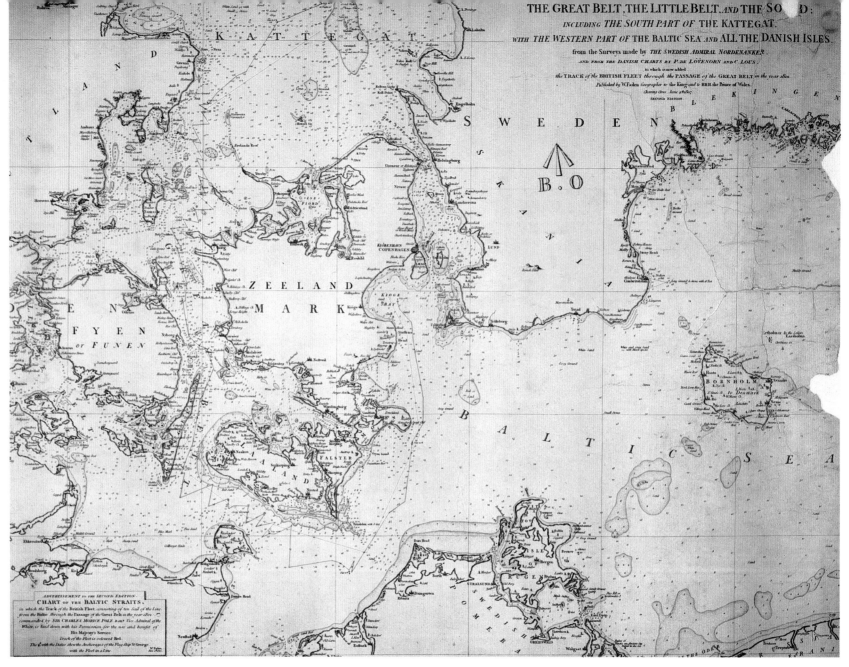

THE GREAT BELT, THE LITTLE BELT, AND THE SOUND;
INCLUDING THE SOUTH PART OF THE KATTEGAT.
WITH THE WESTERN PART OF THE BALTIC SEA AND ALL THE DANISH ISLES
from the Surveys made by THE SWEDISH ADMIRAL NORDENANKER.
AND FROM THE DANISH CHARTS BY P. DE LÖVENORN AND C. LOUS.
to which is now added
the TRACK of the BRITISH FLEET through the PASSAGE of the GREAT BELT in the year 1801.
Published by W. Faden Geographer to the King and to HRH the Prince of Wales.
Coming One June 1780;
SECOND EDITION

Kattegat, 1801

The Royal Navy was Britain's main contribution to the second coalition. Crushing victories at Aboukir Bay and Trafalgar are well recognized, but by the turn of the century British naval forces were involved all over Europe. This map shows, "The track of the British fleet, consisting of ten sail of the line, from the Baltic through the passage of the great belt … commanded by Sir Charles Morice Pole Bart, Vice Admiral of the White." In 1800, angered by Britain's aggressive blockade policy that saw the Royal Navy stop, search, and seize ships and cargoes, Russia, Prussia, Denmark, and Sweden signed a declaration of cooperation against Britain. Known as the Armed Neutrality Agreement, it would last until

1801 and one of its consequences was an attack by the British on Copenhagen. In a typically muscular adventure by the Royal Navy, 26 ships of the line, and 30 other vessels, sailed from England under the command of Admiral Hyde-Parker with Nelson as second-in-command in HMS *Elephant*. In a brilliant action Nelson attacked the Danish navy on 1 April 1801 in its heavily defended Copenhagen anchorage and won a dramatic victory. During the course of the battle Nelson was recalled by Hyde-Parker who thought that the British were beaten. Nelson, who knew otherwise, famously disregarded the order by reading it through his blind eye.

Battle of Marengo, 1800

The final battle in the second coalition's war in Italy—and one of the few battles to have a dish and a horse named after it!—Marengo was Napoleon's great escape and a battle that he had all but lost before General Louis Desaix (1768-1800) arrived in the nick of time. Advancing on a broad front Napoleon had fewer than 18,000 men at hand when he made contact with Austrian General Michael Melas's (1729-1806) forces on the morning of 14 June 1800. Desperately recalling his troops, Napoleon was forced to retreat until Desaix and two divisions arrived. The counterattack was launched and the field won although the cost was higher for the French (some 7,000 casualties) than the Austrians. Numbered among the dead was Desaix, whose arrival had saved Napoleon's army. Napoleon's last horse, Marengo, would survive him by some nine years.

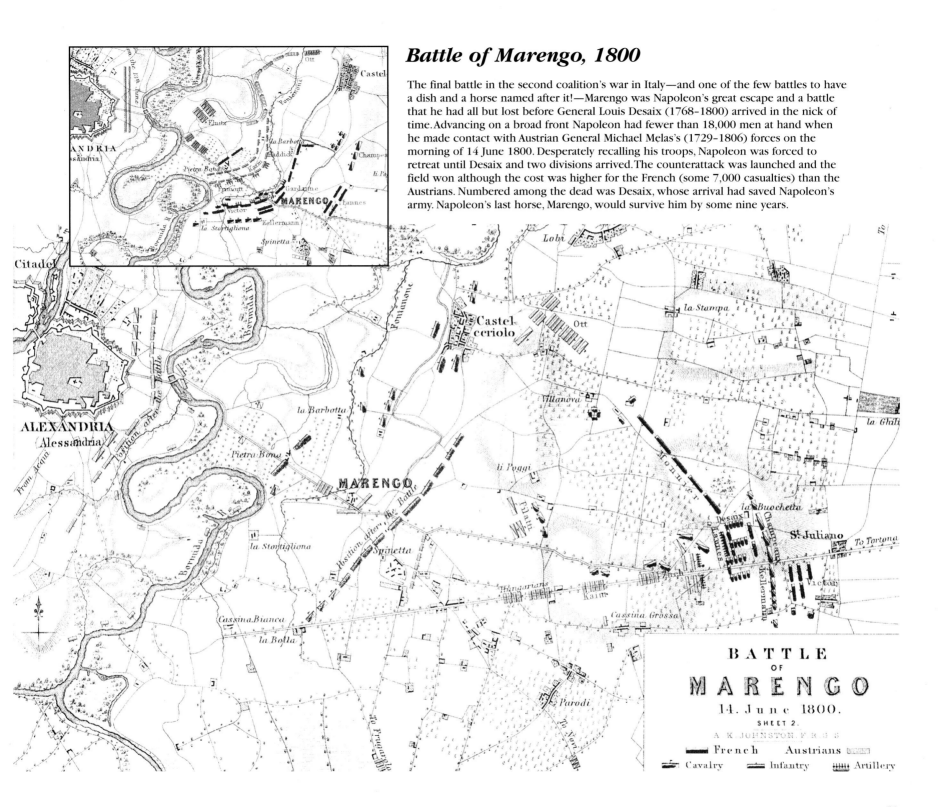

BATTLE
OF
MARENGO
14 June 1800.
SHEET 2.
A K JOHNSTON F.R.G.S

French   Austrians

Cavalry   Infantry   Artillery

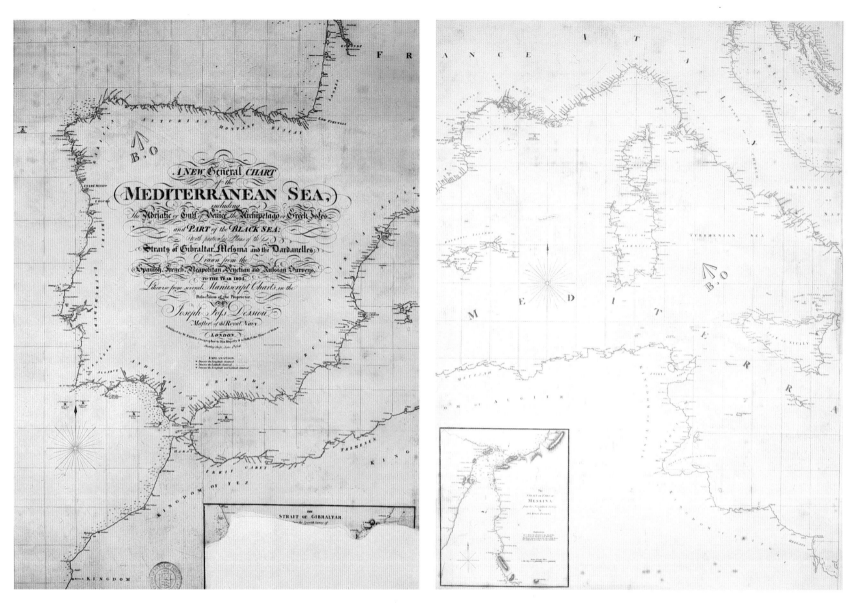

Mediterranean, 1804

"A new general chart of the Mediterranean Sea including the Adriatic or Gulf of Venice, the Archipelago or Greek Isles, and part of the Black Sea: with particular plans of the Straits of Gibraltar, Messina and the Dardanelles: drawn from the Spanish, French, Neapolitan, Venetian and Russian surveys to the year 1804." Published in 1806, this map was produced by Joseph Foss Dessiou, Master of the Royal Navy. Control of the Mediterranean was important to the British for a number of reasons. First, because of its significance as a highway for trade, communications, and international relations. Second, as in World War II, because it allowed the Royal Navy to interrupt enemy supply convoys to theaters such as Egypt. Third, because it allowed them to reinforce Wellington's peninsular army. Fourth, because it allowed Britain to expand its territorial interests. While British naval forces were often overstretched and undermanned, after Nelson's great victories at Aboukir Bay and Trafalgar, the Royal Navy effectively controlled the sea lanes, and the Congress of Vienna confirmed Britain's dominant position by allowing it to keep control of Malta and the Ionian Islands. Note the location of battles including Aboukir Bay.

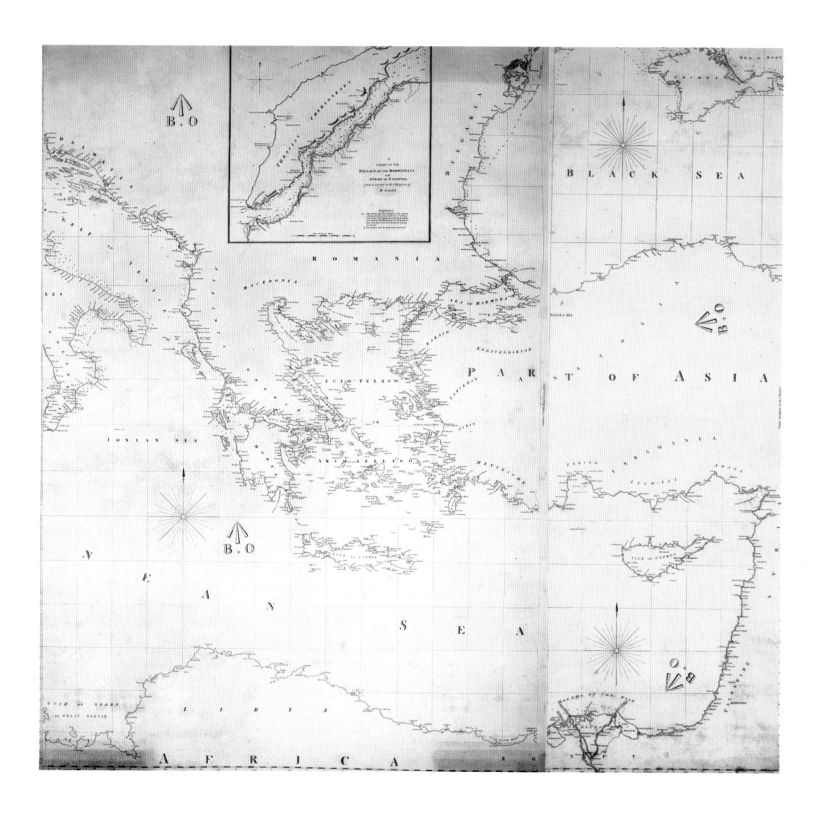

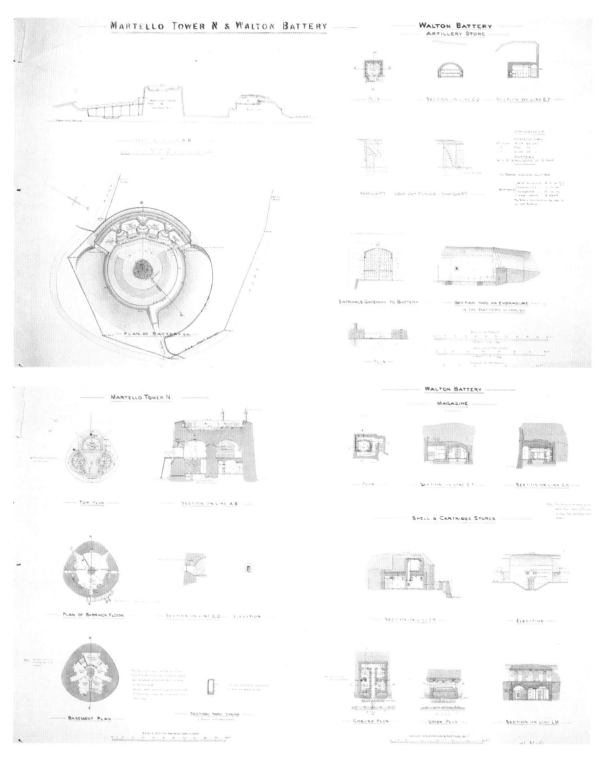

Harwich defenses, 1872

Out of the chronological time sequence of this book, these charts and drawings look at the Martello towers and batteries around Harwich, defenses that were erected in the early part of the 19th century when the threat of a French invasion was at its height. There are five Martello towers on the map, two alongside the Shotleypoint battery, Tower N associated with the Walton battery, and two others on the east coast. The key identifies Tower N as having been built in 1810.

Britain had anticipated an invasion since 1796 when the French had sent a force to invade Ireland. The time of greatest concern was at the end of 1804 when Napoleon had 177,000 men and 2,000 boats ready. Defensive strategy up till this period had not been to deny an enemy a landing but to deter him from using a harbor or proper anchorage. But from 1803 this changed, in no small part because of a frustrated Royal Naval expedition to Corsica that had encountered severe problems from a tower at Mortella Point. Sir David Dundas, who had been involved in this action, proposed a change of strategy: the use of manned towers with two or three big guns to deter an enemy from attempting a landing. Political arguments over cost and likely usefulness led to delays in starting work on the towers until 1805, but by 1808 almost all of 74 towers had been built on the south coast between Folkestone and Seaford. At intervals of 500–600 yards, they were 33 feet high and they had space for a garrison of one officer and 24 men. The east coast towers—including those shown here—were built in 1808-12. In total there were 27 three-gun towers of an improved design between Aldeburgh and St Osyth Stone. Completed in 1810 as well as the Harwich Martello tower was a circular casemate redoubt for ten guns. Other towers were built in Ireland and the Channel Islands, and in all British possessions work took place (see also page 73) to defend British interests.

Antwerp fortifications

Britain was not the only place, of course, where such defensive building took place. These plans, drawn up by British engineers in 1814, show French work around Antwerp.

Below: Plan, sections and elevation of a powder magazine constructed by the French at Antwerp.

Right and Far Right: Plan, sections and elevation of Fort Ferdinand, one of the many forts defending Antwerp, some of which can be seen on the map of the Scheldt on page 60, including Fort Liefkenshoeck (**Far Right**).

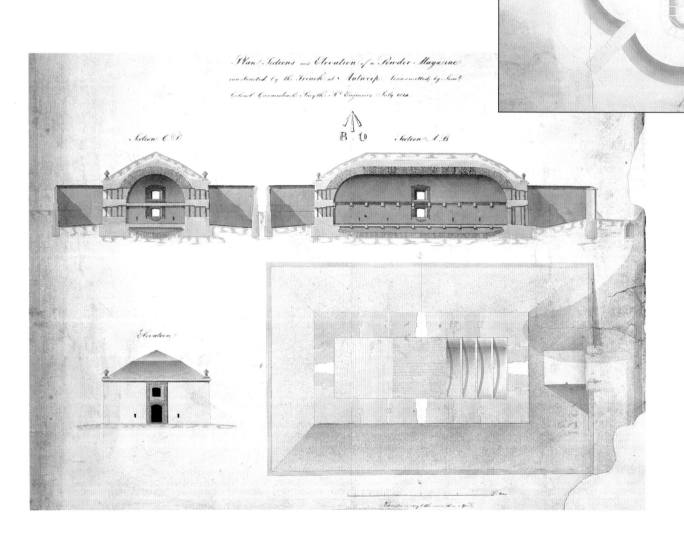

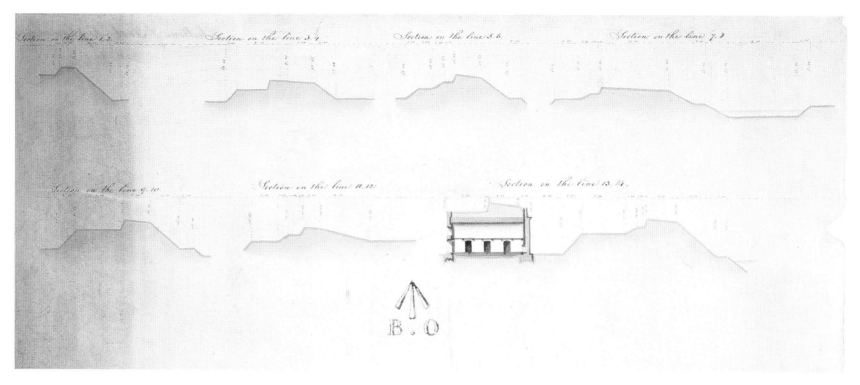

Section on the line 1.2.   Section on the line 3.4.   Section on the line 5.6.   Section on the line 7.8.

Section on the line 9.10.   Section on the line 11.12.   Section on the line 13.14.

B.O

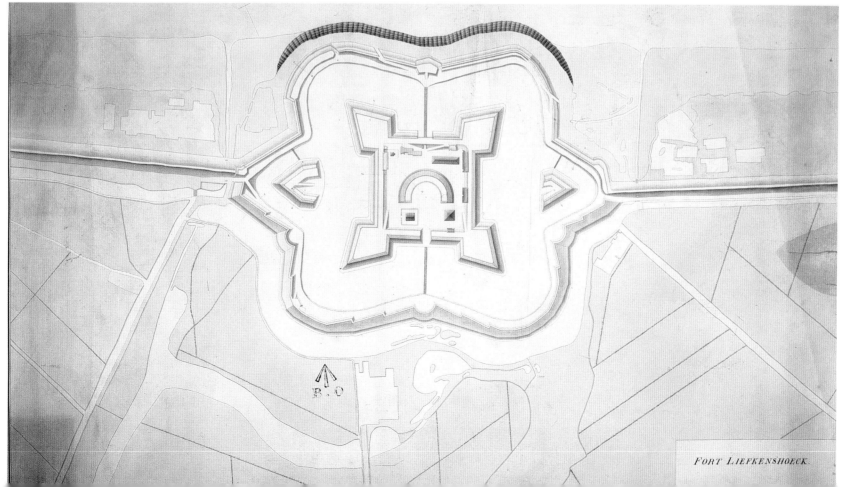

B.O

FORT LIEFKENSHOECK.

Brest Harbor, 1805

Right: Proposed attack on the French fleet using incendiaries. France's most important Atlantic port, Brest was blockaded closely during the war. It was from Brest that the French Atlantic Fleet under Vice-Admiral Honoré Ganteaume (1755–1818) was supposed to escape the blockade as part of Napoleon's complex plan to distract the Royal Navy from its position stopping the invasion of Britain. He was unable to do so and thus left Villeneuve to fight Nelson alone at Trafalgar (see page 61).

Scheldt River, 1805

Below: "A new chart of the River Scheldt from the French survey." Showing the river from its mouth to Antwerp, including Walcheren island and the fortified town of Flushing (see page 85), the chart has been heavily annotated with details of the "Great Expedition" (see page 84).

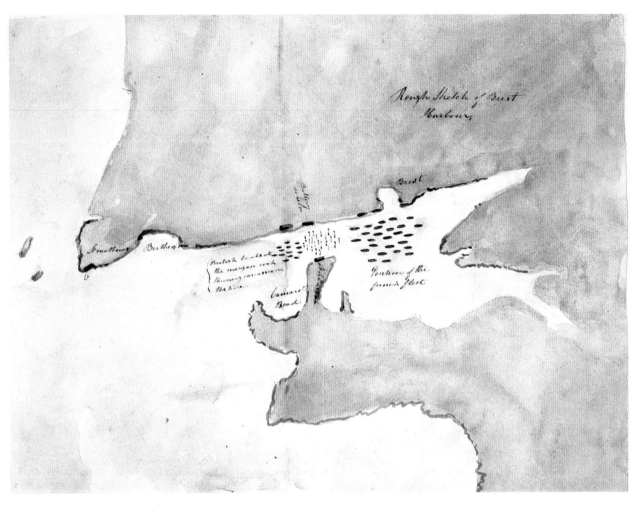

Battle of Trafalgar, 1805

The resounding strategic naval victory of the period, Trafalgar was the last significant naval battle of the Napoleonic wars. With the French fleet beaten, the Royal Navy ruled the waves and was able to constrict Napoleonic Europe in its vice-like grip. The story of Trafalgar was the culmination of the career of the greatest of Britain's naval commanders, Horatio Nelson (1758–1805). Born in Norfolk, son of a clergyman, Nelson started the Napoleonic period as commander of the *Agamemnon*, part of Hood's Mediterranean fleet. An aggressive and inspirational leader, Nelson lost an eye at Calvi during the capture of Corsica in 1794 but this did not stop him playing a major role in the battle of Cape St Vincent in 1797 (see page 42) where he commanded *Captain*. Promoted to rear-admiral and knighted, his next success was at Aboukir Bay (see pages 48–49). It was in Naples, while recovering from head wounds sustained in the battle of the Nile, that he started the affair with Emma Hamilton that was to scandalize contemporary society. He was promoted vice-admiral and became the second-in-command of the punitive mission to Copenhagen in 1801, where his performance won him a peerage. He returned to sea in 1803 as commander of the British fleet in the Mediterranean in a campaign that was to end in posthumous glory at Trafalgar.

This map—"An accurate plan of the three positions of the British fleet before Lord Nelson commenced the action with the combined squadrons of France and Spain on the 21st October 1805"—was drawn by "Mr Ionas Toby, purser of the *Euryalus* who was a spectator of this glorious victory." The story of the battle is well-known: Nelson and his friend and second-in-command, Rear-Admiral Cuthbert Collingwood (1750–1810), led the two battle lines of 11 and 15 battleships respectively into the line of Villeneuve's Combined Fleet. Nelson was killed by a sniper but died knowing that he had won a great victory. Collingwood ably kept his battered fleet together in the teeth of a storm and took over Nelson's position in command of the Mediterranean fleet where he died in service.

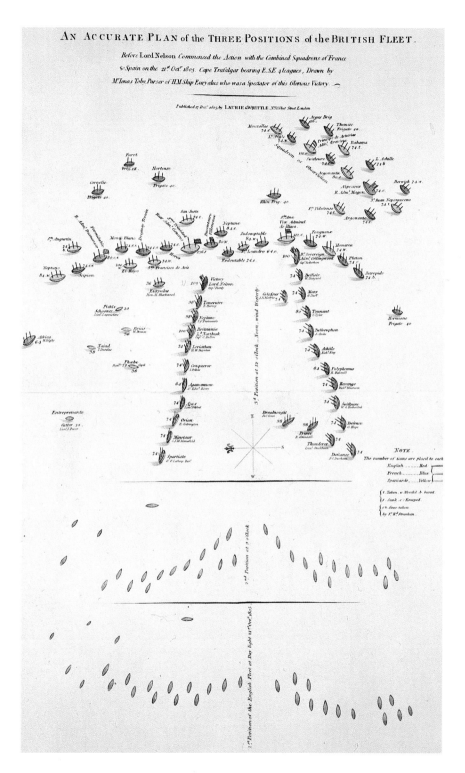

AN ACCURATE PLAN of the THREE POSITIONS of the BRITISH FLEET.

Before Lord Nelson Commenced the Action with the Combined Squadrons of France & Spain on the 21st Oct.r 1805. Cape Trafalgar bearing E.S.E 4 leagues, Drawn by Mr Ionas Toby, Purser of HM Ship Euryalus who was a Spectator of this Glorious Victory.

France's Eastern border, 1805

"Fairburn's Map of the scene of actions on the German, French, Dutch, Swiss, and Italian borders exhibiting at one view the whole theater of war from the Mediterranean Sea to Dutch Brabant and Gelders including the Rivers Rhine, Po, Danube, Neckar, Mayne, Lhan, Moselle, Meuse, etc." The third edition of this map, it was published on 21 October 1805, the same day as the battle of Trafalgar. This copy was found in the papers of William Pitt the Younger (1759-1806) who was prime minister of Great Britain from 1783 (aged only 23) to 1801 and then again from 1804 to his death in 1806. In the map the boundary of Germany is in red; that of Dutch territory in purple; France in yellow; Switzerland in Orange; and Italy in green. The year 1805 saw the start of the war of the third coalition (Austria, Britain, Naples, Russia, Sweden, a number of German states, and, latterly, Prussia) against the now emperor Napoleon. Crushing Napoleonic victories at Ulm in Bavaria (20 October 1805) and Austerlitz in Moravia (2 December 1805) saw France victorious on land; defeat at Trafalgar, however, meant that the Royal Navy's control of the sea rendered Napoleon unable to attack his bitter foe, Great Britain.

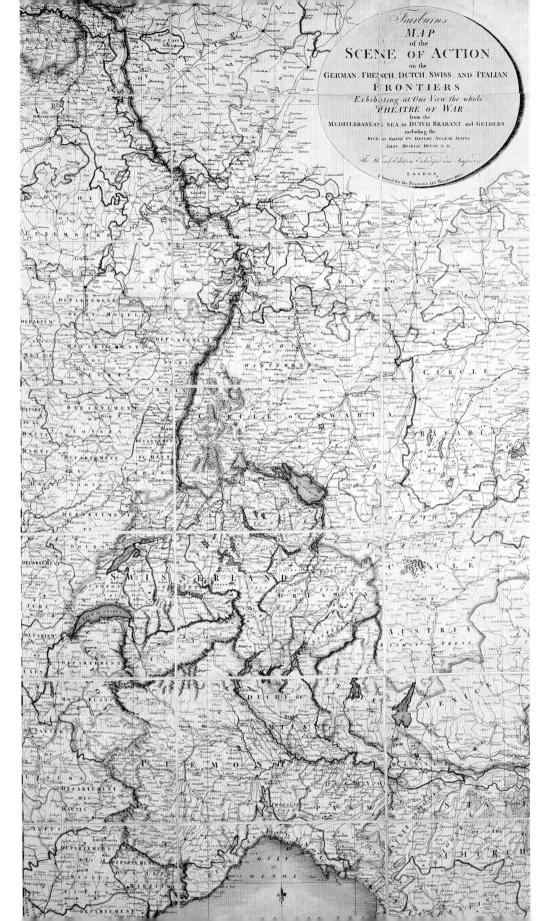

Battle of Maida, 1806

"Plan of the battle of Maida fought on the plains of St Eufemia in Calabria Ulteriore on the ever memorable day July 4 1806 by a small British force of 4795 men under the command of Major General Sir J. Stuart KB against a superior French force consisting of 7,800 men under the orders of General Regnier in which the former gained a most signal victory."

Italy south of the Papal States and Sicily had been one kingdom— the Kingdom of the Two Sicilies— since 1738, ruled by the Spanish Bourbons. In 1759 Ferdinand IV of Naples (and III of Sicily) took the throne. Naples joined the first coalition and, following the collapse of the coalition and French successes in the north, attacked the French by itself, urged on by Horatio Nelson who had been recuperating in Naples following the battle of the Nile (see page 61). The Neapolitan campaign was a disaster and ended with the French occupying Naples in 1799. In 1805, when Ferdinand supported the third coalition, Napoleon placed his elder brother, Joseph Bonaparte (1768-1844), on the throne. In spite of British resistance to this and British success at Maida, the French were able to consolidate their position in Naples, although Sicily remained free. When Joseph—who had ruled well— abdicated to become king of Spain, his position was taken by General Joachim Murat (1767-1815), who had married Caroline Bonaparte (1782-1839), Napoleon's youngest sister. Ferdinand was reinstated to the throne by the Congress of Vienna.

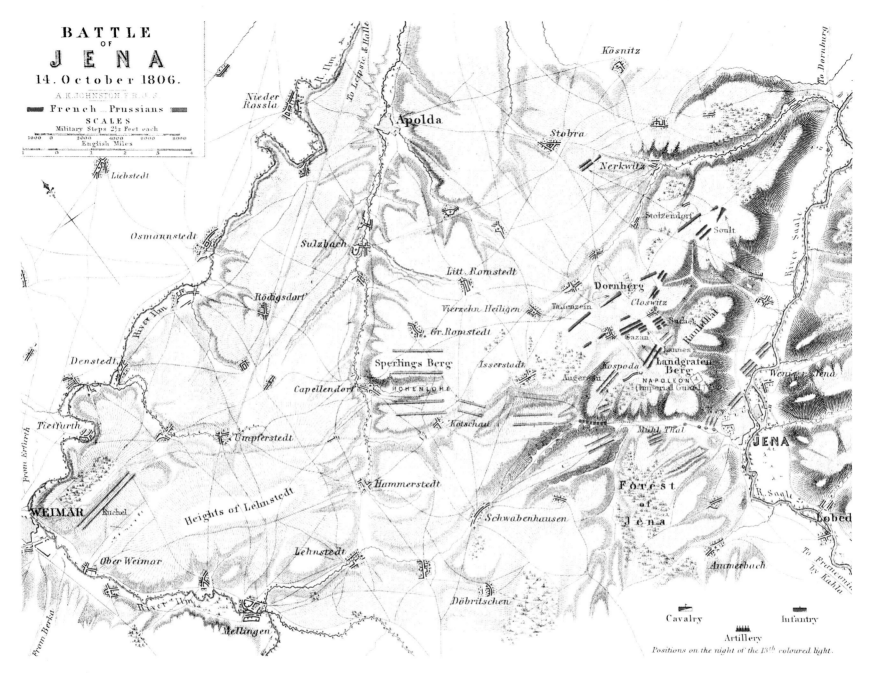

Positions on the night of the 13th coloured light.

Cavalry   Infantry

Artillery

Battle of Jena, 1806

In autumn 1806 came the war of the fourth coalition (Prussia, Russia, and Britain). It started when Prussia declared war on France. It was ended in July 1807 by the Peace of Tilsit following French victories at Jena, Auerstädt (page 65), Eylau (page 66), and Friedland (page 67). The first part of this, the Jena-Auerstädt campaign of autumn 1806, saw Napoleon defeat the southern part of the Prussian army at Jena on 14 October 1806—losing some 5,000 men, as against the Prussians' 10,000, and taking 15,000 prisoners.

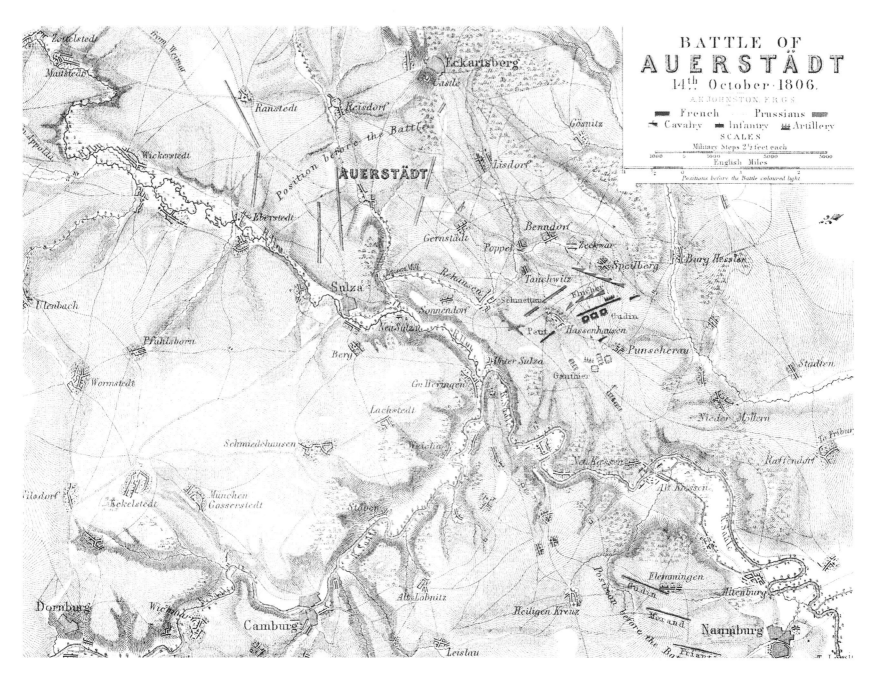

Battle of Auerstädt, 1806

The other engagement that took place on 14 October was the battle of Auerstädt. This saw French Marshal Louis Davout's (1770–1823) 27,000-man III Corps hold off the main Prussian Army—63,000 men under the Duke of Brunswick—inflicting 10,000 casualties as against 7,000 French and taking 3,000 prisoners along with 115 guns. It was a brilliant victory and one that confirmed Davout as one of Napoleon's best fighting marshals. He had close ties to Napoleon through his marriage to the sister of Pauline Bonaparte's husband Leclerc. Davout commanded the right wing at Austerlitz and after his successes he was created duc d'Auerstädt in 1808. In 1809, following the battle of Eckmühl, he became prince of Eckmühl. He fought with distinction at Wagram, held Hamburg in 1813–14 and was Napoleon's War Minister and Governor of Paris in 1815 during the Hundred Days.

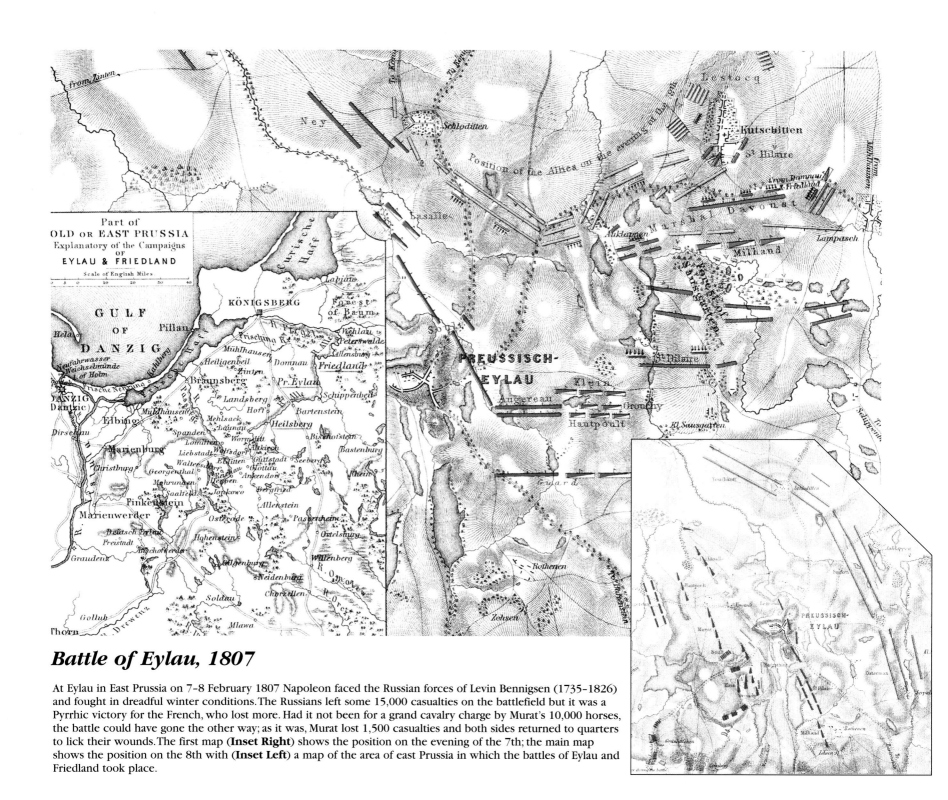

Battle of Eylau, 1807

At Eylau in East Prussia on 7–8 February 1807 Napoleon faced the Russian forces of Levin Bennigsen (1735–1826) and fought in dreadful winter conditions. The Russians left some 15,000 casualties on the battlefield but it was a Pyrrhic victory for the French, who lost more. Had it not been for a grand cavalry charge by Murat's 10,000 horses, the battle could have gone the other way; as it was, Murat lost 1,500 casualties and both sides returned to quarters to lick their wounds. The first map (**Inset Right**) shows the position on the evening of the 7th; the main map shows the position on the 8th with (**Inset Left**) a map of the area of east Prussia in which the battles of Eylau and Friedland took place.

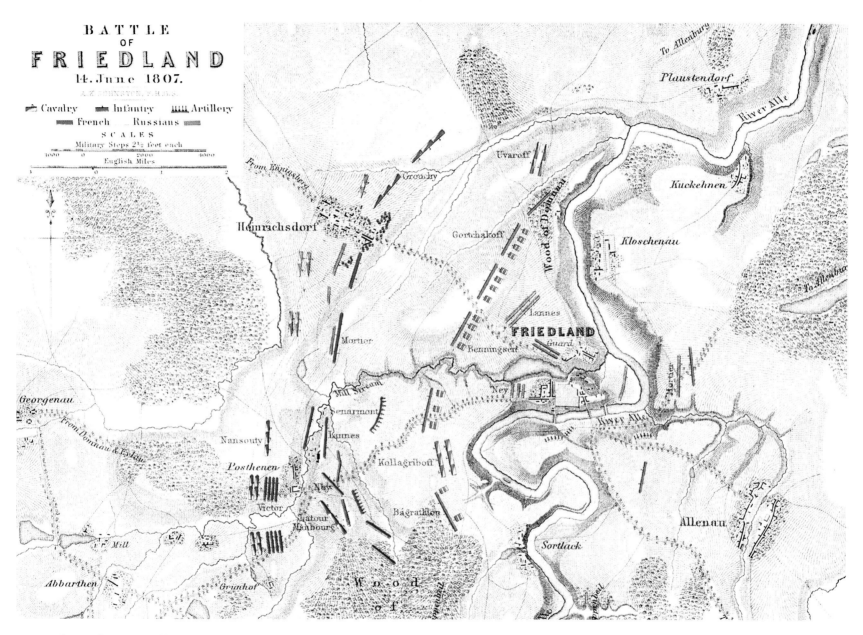

Battle of Friedland, 1807

On 14 June Napoleon finished the Russians off, losing 10,000 men in the process but inflicting twice as many casualties on Bennigsen's army and forcing Tsar Alexander I (1777–1825) to negotiate the Peace of Tilsit, and thus end the war of the fourth coalition.

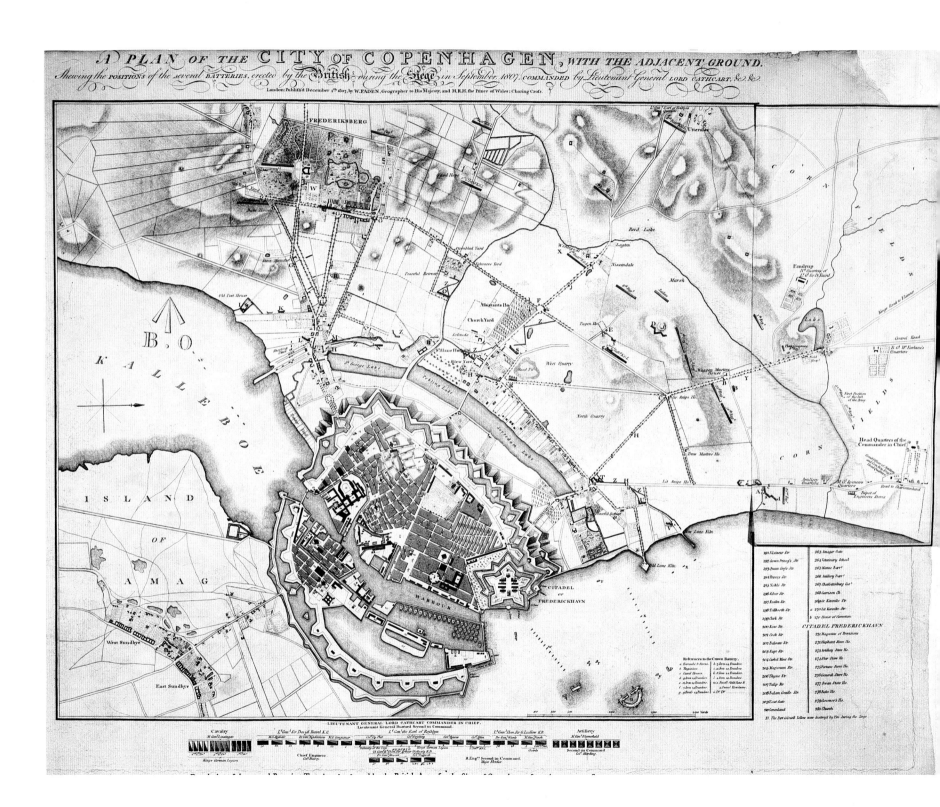

A PLAN OF THE CITY OF COPENHAGEN, WITH THE ADJACENT GROUND.

Shewing the POSITIONS of the several BATTERIES, erected by the British, during the Siege in September, 1807, COMMANDED by Lieutenant General LORD CATHCART, &c. &c.

London: Publish'd December 1st 1807, by W. FADEN, Geographer to His Majesty, and H.R.H. the Prince of Wales; Charing Cross.

68

Battle of Copenhagen, 1807

"A plan of the city of Copenhagen with the adjacent ground showing the position of the several batteries erected by the British during the siege in September 1807 commanded by Lt-General Lord Cathcart."

As part of its contribution to the war of the fourth coalition, Britain sent a fleet of 25 warships—together with nearly 30,000 men under Lord Cathcart (including in their number Major-General Arthur Wellesley)—on a preemptive attack on neutral Denmark. The rationale behind the attack was that France was putting pressure on Denmark to ally with her against the coalition, and that the British blockade of Europe had led to friction. The British bombarded the Danish fleet in Copenhagen harbor and invested the city. Some 2,000 civilians died and although the British gained 17 warships and some £2 million, the action had a massively damaging effect on Britain's reputation in Europe and America. Indeed, it was to be the heavy-handed blockading of mercantile interests that would eventually bring Britain and the United States to war in 1812 (see pages 120-123).

Right: Two sketches of Copenhagen and the ground gained in August 1807.

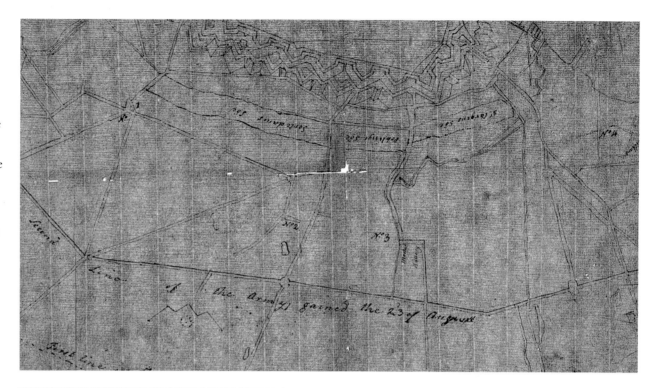

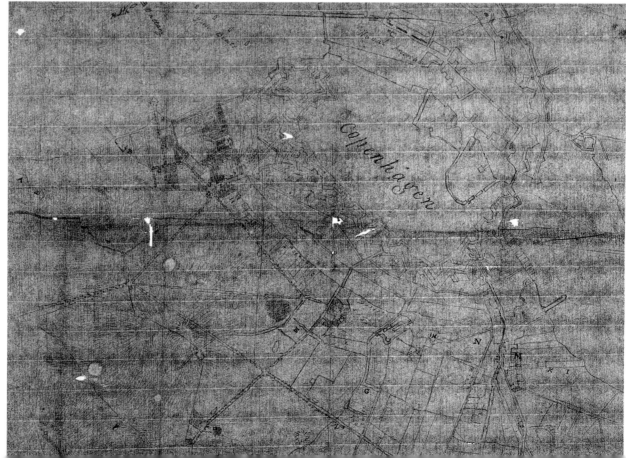

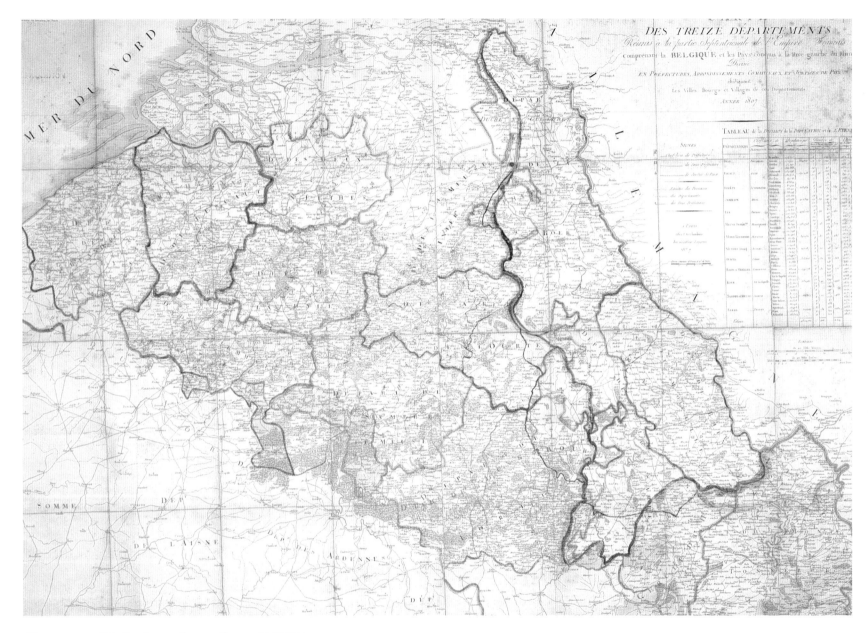

Franco-Belgian border, 1807

"Map of the 13 departments reunited to the French Empire comprising Belgium, and the land conquered on the left bank of the Rhine." Can there be an area that has seen more fighting in the last 300 years than the northern and northeastern border of France? Flanders, Belgium, and Alsace-Lorraine have been battlefields so often and have been lost and reunited countless times. The Congress of Vienna set the boundaries of France back to those in 1792.

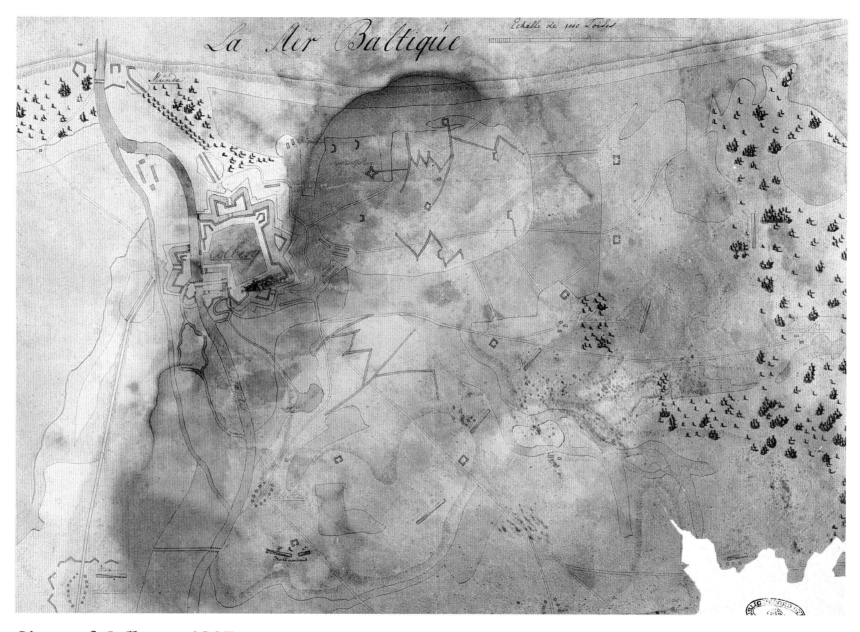

La Mir Baltique

Echelle de 1000 Toises

Siege of Colberg, 1807

Poland, for long a bastion of the west against enemies from the east—King Jan Sobieski had been the savior of Europe when he saved Vienna from the Turks in 1683—by the 19th century was weak and threatened by its neighbors. As the map on page 141 shows, Poland was partitioned—in other words split up between its neighbors—three times in the late 18th century and would continue to be fought over in the 19th and 20th centuries. Indeed, Napoleon was welcomed by the inhabitants when he occupied Prussian Poland in late 1806 and then created the Duchy of Warsaw at Tilsit as it was felt that he could protect Poland from its neighbors. During the campaign in Poland, Colberg (now Kolobrzeg) was besieged from 20 March to 2 July 1807.

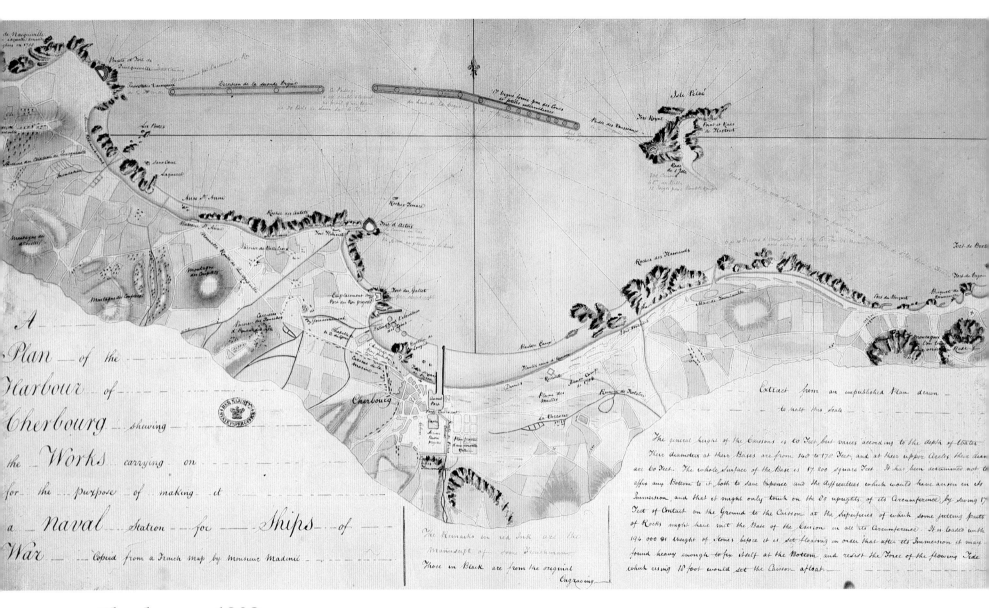

Cherbourg, 1808

"A plan of the harbor of Cherbourg showing works carrying on for the purpose of making it a naval station for war." Copied from a French map—the marginal note identifies that remarks in red are the manuscript of "some Frenchman"— Cherbourg was one of many ports along France's Channel coast that were strengthened both in the run up to a possible invasion of Britain and also to defend shipping from the depredations of the Royal Navy.

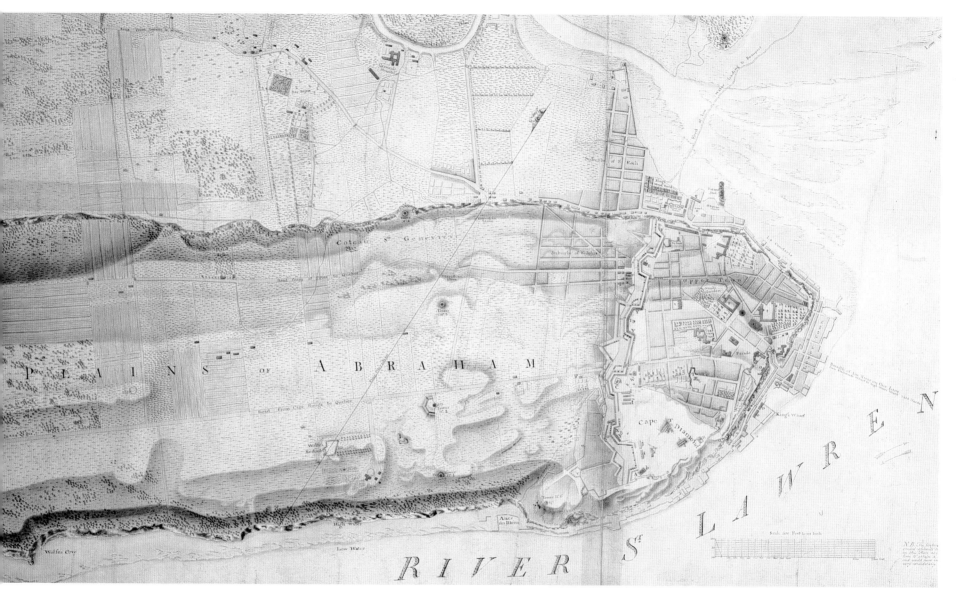

Quebec, 1808

"Plan of the town and fortifications of Quebec including the works that are now carrying on to increase the defenses of the place, July 1808." The war against Napoleon was a world war and the British naval blockade—enforced rigorously on enemy and neutral shipping—was a bone of contention that would eventually lead the United States and Britain into war. Quebec was an important strategic location and as such needed to be sure of its defenses—after all, British forces under Wolfe had themselves stormed and taken the city only a few years earlier in 1759.

Portugal, 1808

Above Right: Napoleon, flushed with a successful conclusion to the war of the fourth coalition in 1807, decided to take Spain and Portugal, a long-time ally of Britain. He assumed that—as elsewhere in Europe—French order would be greeted by the people of the area: he could not have been more wrong. The war that ensued—the Peninsular War—would suck troops away from elsewhere in the empire, lead to over 300,000 French casualties and, ultimately, the work of the British and Spanish forces would be instrumental in bringing Napoleon down. This map shows the movements of British troops from Mondego Bay to Vimeiro.

Battle of Vimeiro, 1808

Below Right and Far Right: Two plans of the battle—the first major engagement of the war—that took place on 21 August 1808 between Generals Arthur Wellesley and Andoche Junot (1771-1813), the latter the invader of Portugal in 1807 and, as the Duc d'Abrantès, its governor. Vimeiro saw a smaller French force (some 13,000 men) attempt to take 15,000 by surprise. The British victory had little short term effect, other than to—temporarily—free Portugal; what it did do was establish the credentials of the general who would ultimately defeat Napoleon, show the benefit of his tactics and the abilities of his fighting men. The first is portrayed with north at the top; the second with north at the bottom.

Map illustrative of
THE MILITARY MOVEMENTS IN
PORTUGAL
in July and August 1808,
referred to in the Life of
FIELDMARSHAL THE DUKE OF
WELLINGTON.

By A. Petermann, F.R.G.S.

Scale of English Miles.

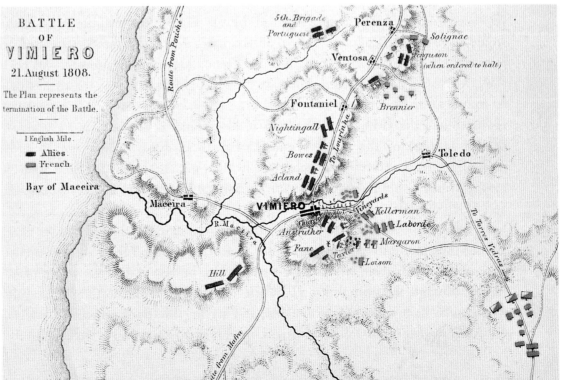

BATTLE
OF
VIMIERO
21. August 1808.

The Plan represents the termination of the Battle.

1 English Mile.
■ Allies.
▬ French.

Bay of Maceira

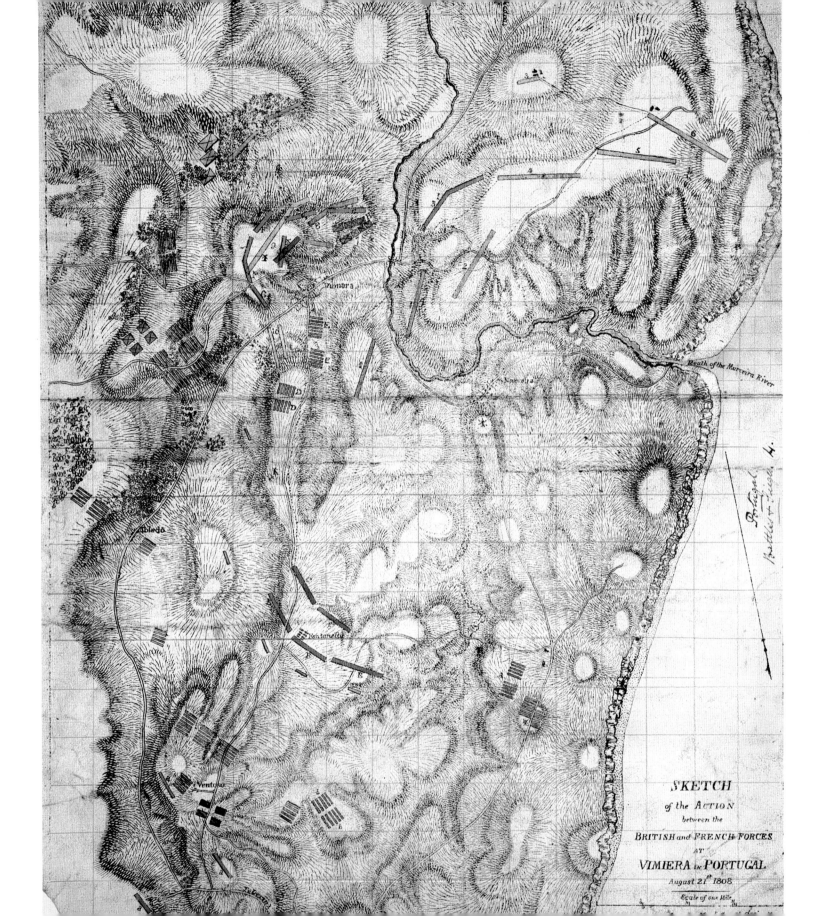

SKETCH
of the ACTION
between the
BRITISH and FRENCH FORCES
AT
VIMIERA in PORTUGAL
August 21st 1808

Scale of one Mile

Mouth of the Maceira River

Vimeira

75

Portugal, 1809

Following the debacle of Sir John Moore's defeat and death at the end of 1808 (albeit with a Dunkirk-like evacuation of most of the British force at Coruña), command of the Peninsular army was given to Wellesley, who returned to Lisbon from Britain on 22 April with 25,000 men, joining the 16,000 or so already on the Iberian Peninsula. Wellington trained his army and reorganized it and then marched toward Oporto. These maps show the movements of Wellington's army in May 1809 leading to the passage of the Douro at Oporto on 12 May.

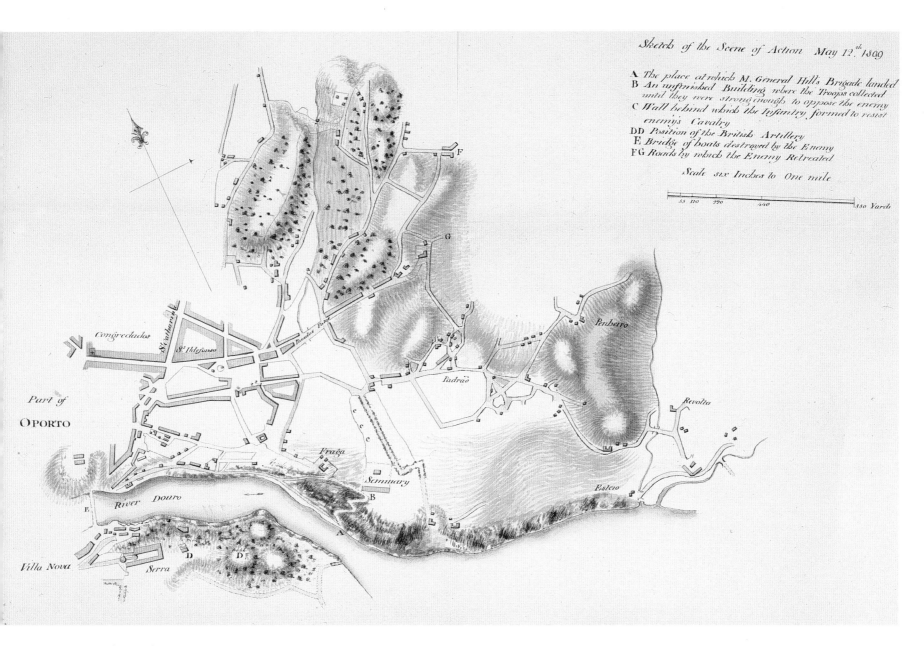

Sketch of the Scene of Action May 12.th 1809

A The place at which M. General Hills Brigade landed
B An unfinished Building where the Troops collected
    until they were strong enough to oppose the enemy
C Wall behind which the Infantry formed to resist
    enemy's Cavalry
DD Position of the British Artillery
E Bridge of boats destroyed by the Enemy
FG Roads by which the Enemy Retreated

Scale six Inches to One mile

55 110   270   440   880 Yards

Congreclados
S.t Catherine
S.ta Ildefonso
Paradas Pa...
Penheiro
Part of
OPORTO
Padraõ
Revolta
Fraga
Seminary
B
Estero
River Douro
E
A
Villa Nova
Serra
D D

Battle of Oporto, 1809

A view of the crossing of the Douro that led to the taking of Oporto, the spring-board for Wellesley's invasion of Spain. Some 18,500 troops—2,500 of them Portuguese—had marched with Wellesley to Oporto where the enemy had concentrated their defenses on the seaward side of the town and left the river unguarded. The British crossed the river, surprised the garrison and then moved east toward Talavera.

Central Europe, 1809

Map showing the area of conflict of the war of the fifth coalition in 1809, from Ulm (site of a great Napoleonic victory in October 1805) on the left to Vienna on the right. It was to the northeast of Vienna on 5–6 July that the huge battle of Wagram took place. It ended the war in a French victory that would lead to the Treaty of Schönbrunn.

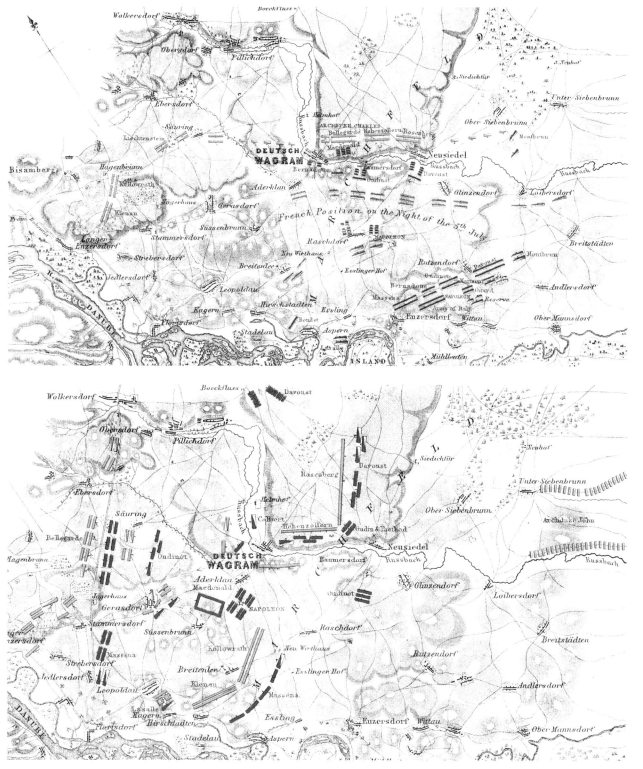

Battle of Wagram, 1809

The war of the fifth coalition saw Austria take up the cudgels in April 1809 and join Britain against Napoleon. It ended for Austria on 5–6 July with the bloody battle of Wagram that saw over 70,000 casualties. The French themselves lost over 32,500 killed or wounded including 40 generals. There were other casualties—French Marshal Jean-Baptiste Bernadotte (see page 114) was dismissed from the army for the poor handling of his corps. While Austrian Archduke Charles managed to retreat with his force intact, around 40,000 casualties weakened him considerably—somuchso that on 10 July he was defeated again at Znaim and forced to sign an armistice on the 12th. Britain would continue fighting, in the Iberian peninsula and also in northwest Europe in the form of the ill-advised Walcheren expedition (see page 84). The two maps show (**Above**) the position on the 5th and (**Below**) the 6th.

Battle of Talavera, 1809

After his success at Oporto, Wellesley advanced into Spain and met a much larger force under Jourdan. As was to become the hallmark of his campaign in the Peninsula, Wellington's force gained a victory through training and discipline and the quality of its defensive positions. While the victory led to Wellesley becoming Lord Wellington, it didn't achieve any strategic benefits and Wellington was forced to retreat toward Lisbon as French forces under Ney and Soult advanced. These excellent maps and those on pages 82–83 show various views and stages of the battle:

Above Right: The movements of the forces toward Talavera and after the battle, 25 July–3 August.

Below Right: Positions of the armies toward the close of the battle of 27-28 July.

Far Right: Another view of the battle.

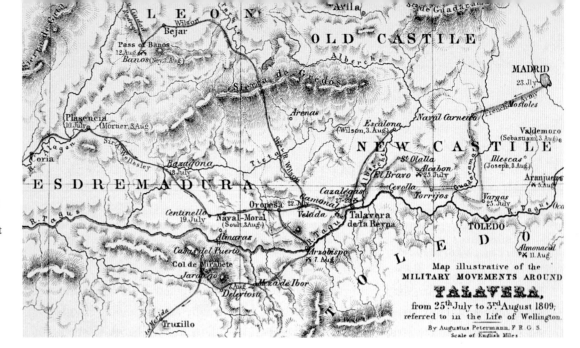

Map illustrative of the
MILITARY MOVEMENTS AROUND
TALAVERA,
from 25th July to 3rd August 1809;
referred to in the Life of Wellington.
By Augustus Petermann, F.R.G.S.
Scale of English Miles

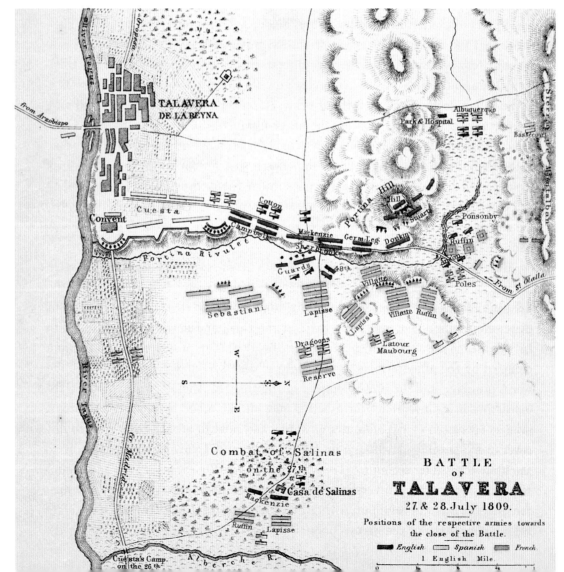

BATTLE
OF
TALAVERA
27. & 28. July 1809.
Positions of the respective armies towards
the close of the Battle.

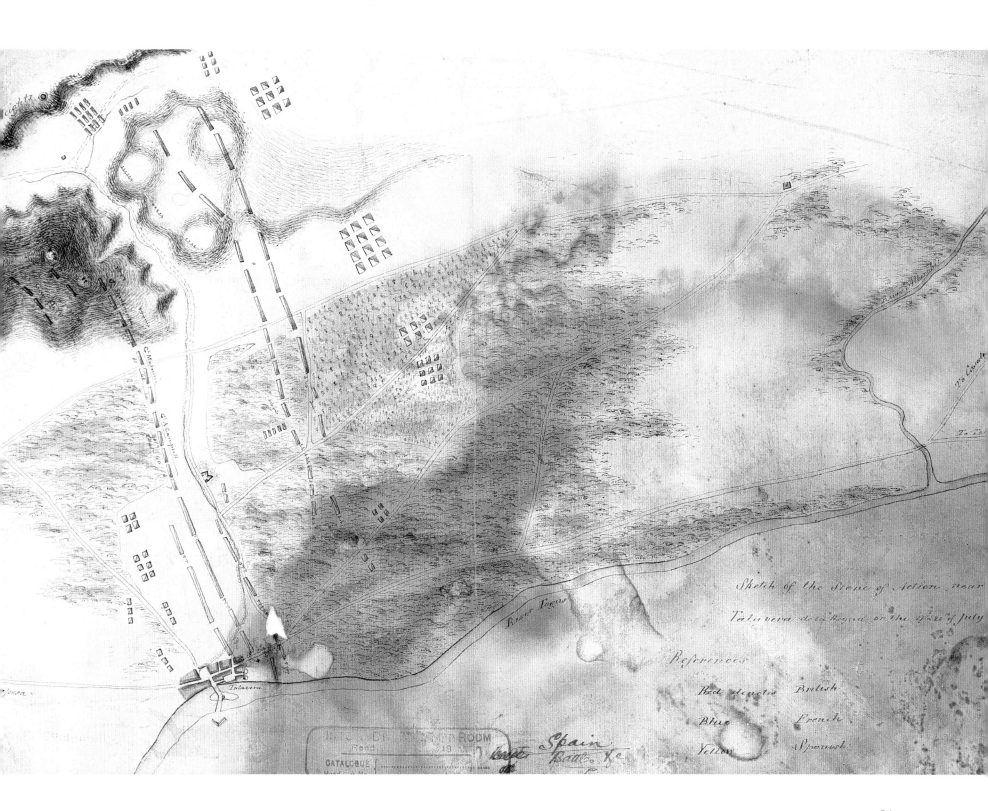

Sketch of the Scene of Action near

Talavera de la Reyna on the 27 & 28 of July

References

Red denotes British

Blue French

Yellow Spanish

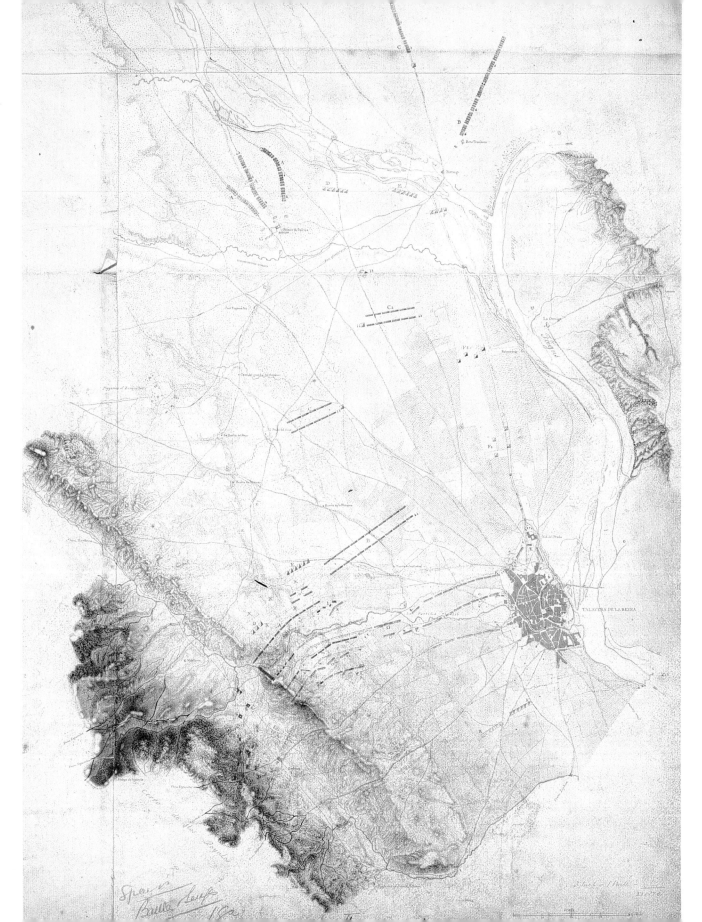

Right: A different angle of the field of battle at Talavera.

Far Right: The battlefield from a sketch by Lt-Col Fletcher.

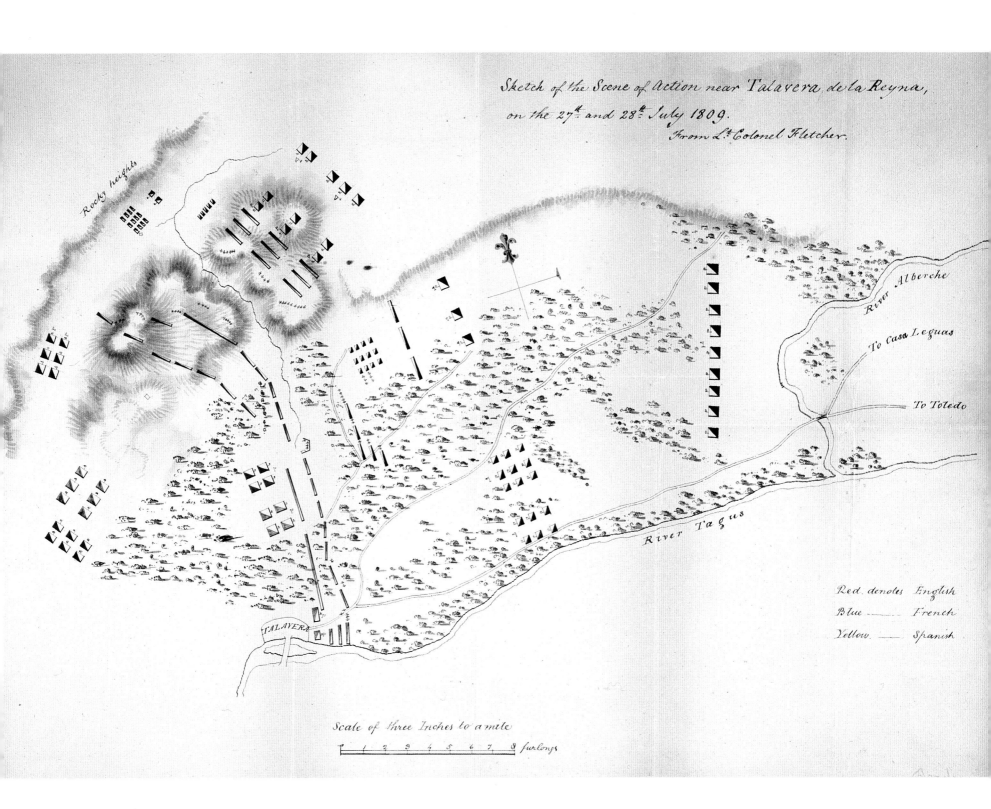

Sketch of the Scene of Action near Talavera, de la Reyna,
on the 27th and 28th July 1809.
From Lt. Colonel Fletcher.

Rocky heights

River Alberche

To Casa Leguas

To Toledo

River Tagus

TALAVERA

Red denotes English
Blue ——— French
Yellow ——— Spanish

Scale of three Inches to a mile

0 1 2 3 4 5 6 7 8 furlongs

83

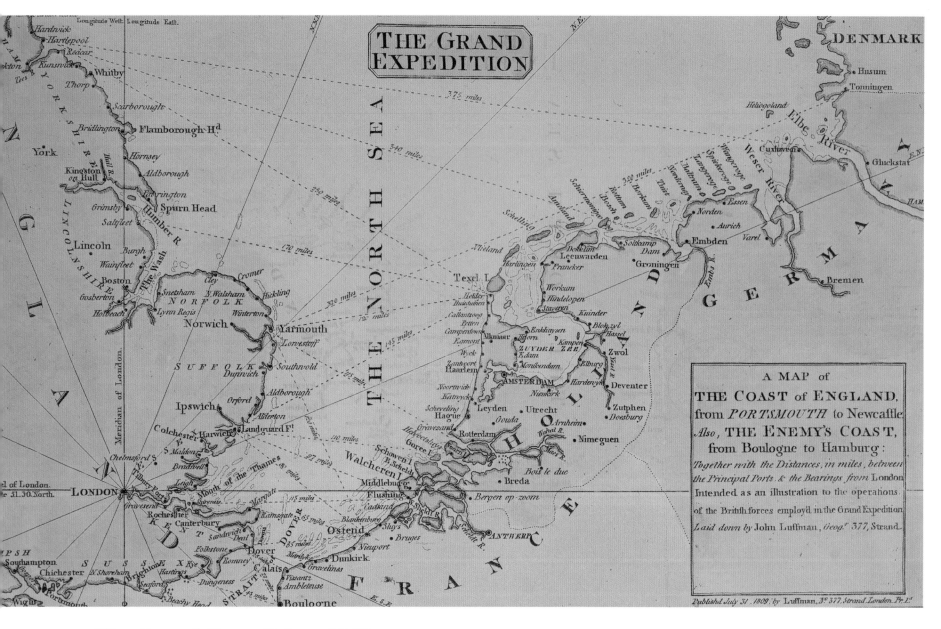

The Grand Expedition, 1809

"A map of the coast of England from Portsmouth to Newcastle and the enemy's coast from Boulogne to Hamburg: together with the distances, in miles, between the principal ports and the bearings from London intended as an illustration to the operations of the British forces employed in the Great Expedition."

Published 31 July 1809 by John Luffman, geographer, this shows the area surrounding the island of Walcheren that was invaded by British forces at the

end of July 1809—Britain's ill-conceived and extremely tardy contribution to the war of the fifth coalition. Over a million pounds were expended on a campaign that did little more than reduce top-line regiments to skeletons of their former selves and reduce morale accordingly. That it took place at all, after the defeat of the Austrians at Wagram (see page 79), was the result of a military and political juggernaut that could not be halted in time.

Siege of Flushing, 1809

"Plan of the siege of Flushing by the army under the command of Lt-Gen the Earl of Chatham KG." The only military success of the invasion was the successful siege of Flushing, that fell on 15 August. A combination of disease and poor management led to the expedition's complete failure and the troops who survived—there were 17,000 casualties—were taken off by the Royal Navy from 14 September, the rearguard finally being extracted on 24 December.

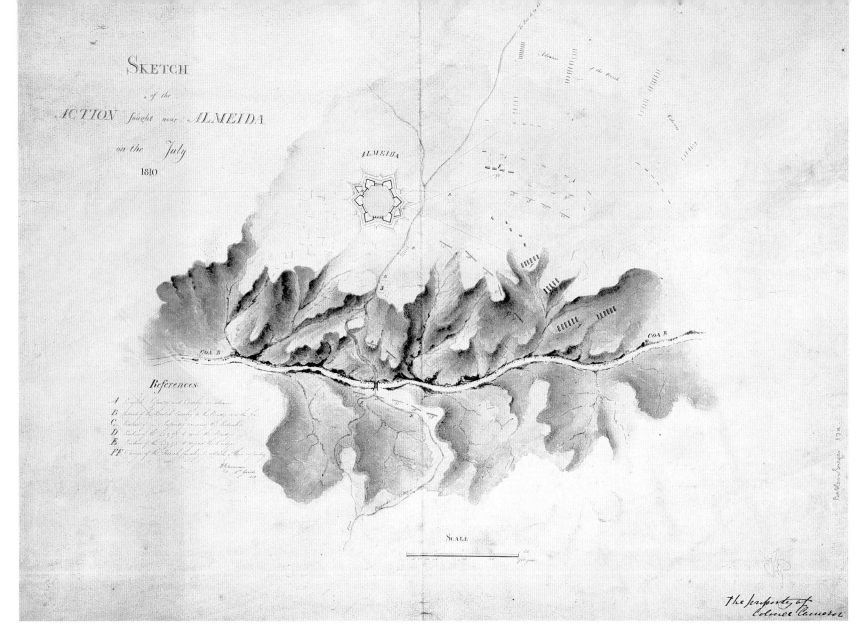

Battle of Almeida, 1810

Sketch of the battle fought on 24 July by the Light Division (including two Portuguese units) under Robert Crauford against the French under Ney. It shows the French advancing on the British more quickly than Crauford expected; the dash to save the cavalry and guns as the infantry covered the retreat; and the British positions defending the bridge. What it doesn't show is the slaughter when Ney pushed his men to cross the Coa in the face of the guns of the Light Division and two of the best British regiments involved in the Peninsular War—the 43rd Monmouthshire Light Infantry and the Rifle Corps, the 95th. Also involved were Portuguese troops—a major component of Wellington's Army, comprising around a third of his field troops. From 9 March 1809 the Portuguese army was commanded by William Beresford (1768-1854) with the rank of

marshal. A top administrator, he transformed what had been a weak and poorly-led army into a significant force that would contribute materially to Wellington's successes. Ney would send his superior, Massena, a truthful account of the events at Almeida but Massena would write it up for Napoleon as a French victory. The key reads:

A   English infantry and cavalry in advance.
B   Retreat of the British cavalry to the bridge across the Coa.
C   Position of our infantry covering the retreat.
D   Position of the 95th and 43rd [Regiments] to cover the bridge.
E   Position of the 95th and 43rd [Regiments] to defend the bridge.
F   Charge of the French cavalry.

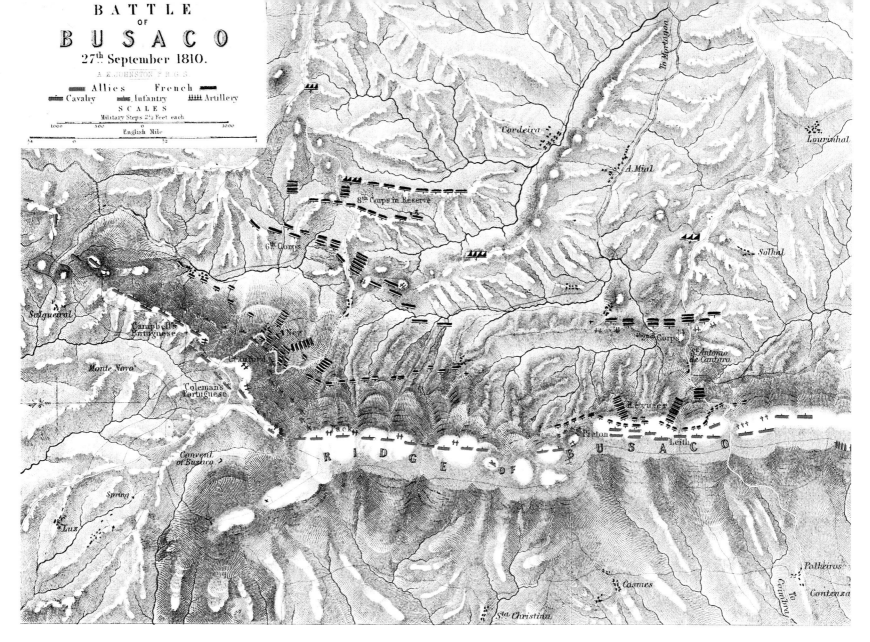

Battle of Busaco, 1810

Fought on 27 September 1810 the battle of Busaco typified Wellington's strategy in this period. As he retreated back into Portugal toward winter quarters he was pursued by Massena whose forces outnumbered him. He ensured, therefore, that the battle took place on ground of his choosing, with his 25,000 British and 25,000 Portuguese troops in excellent defensive positions along the ridge of Busaco. The French frontal attacks did little damage to the British and Sir Charles Oman in his history records the casualties: 1,252 to the Allies, of whom 200 were killed, and an incomplete French casualty return noted 4,498 casualties including 522 killed, the number including a general (Graindorge) and 54 officers—the high proportion of officers being due to their desperate attempts made to push the French attacks on. That the British line held was in no small part due to the role of Thomas Picton (1758-1815) of the 3rd Division, who would die in the thick of the action at Waterloo.

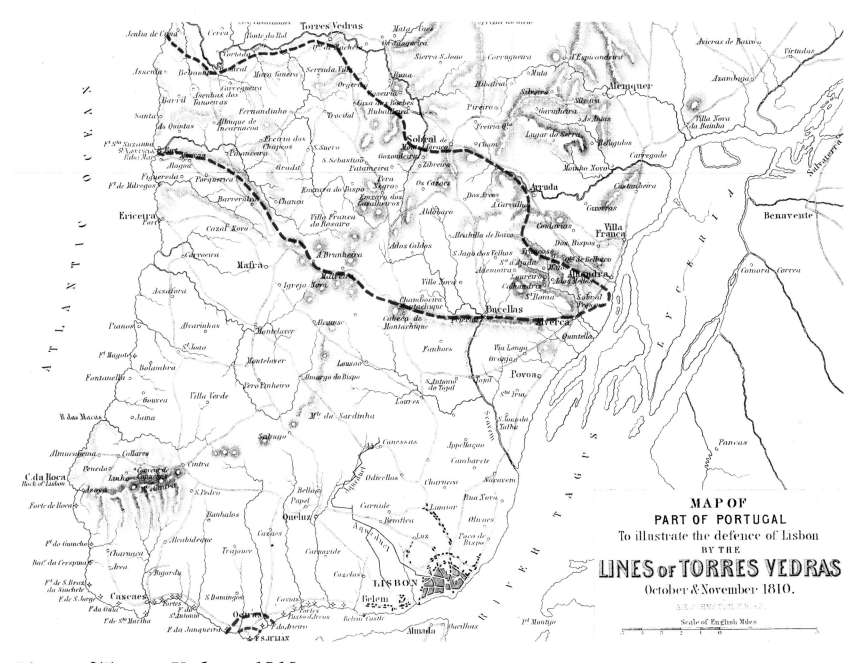

MAP OF
PART OF PORTUGAL
To illustrate the defence of Lisbon
BY THE
LINES of TORRES VEDRAS
October & November 1810.

A.K. JOHNSTON, F.R.S.E.

Scale of English Miles

Lines of Torres Vedras, 1810

Wellington's winter quarters were behind the lines of Torres Vedras in Portugal. Well appointed, using the sea and the River Tagus—on which the Royal Navy placed a patrolling flotilla of 14 gunboats—as natural fortifications, the lines were in fact a series of defended redoubts, over 150 of them, with only short distances of wall. Behind the lines roads were built to allow rapid redeployment of troops in defense and there was an excellent semaphore signalling system to allow speedy communications between the redoubts. Wellington had started their construction by a secret order to his chief engineer, Lt-Col Sir Richard Fletcher (1768–1813). The lines proved impenetrable to Massena as he followed Wellington's army after Busaco. Massena retired to winter quarters at Santarem (see page 90) telling Napoleon that a major attack was pointless. Guerillas, disease and hunger would cause Massena many problems over the forthcoming months, while the British enjoyed the pleasures of good supplies and fox-hunting behind their defenses.

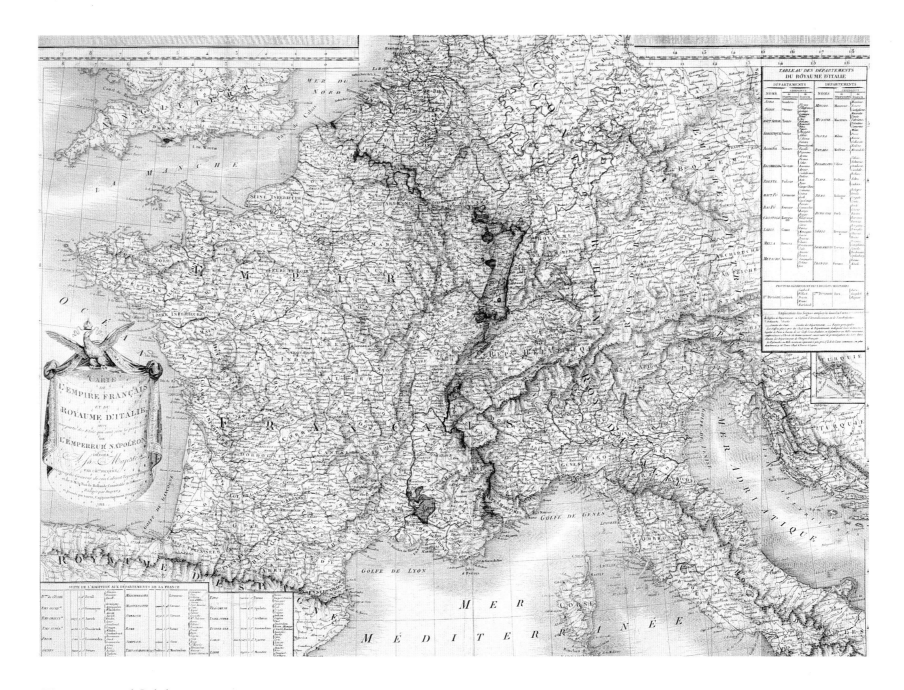

Europe, 1811

"Map of the French Empire and Kingdom of Italy with some of the states that are under the protection of the Emperor Napoleon." Panels identify the additional departments of France (lower left) and the departments of the kingdom of Italy (right). Europe in 1811 was in the thrall of Napoleon, with his rule, or that of his family, spreading from Spain in the west to Illyria in the east; from Holland in the north to Italy in the south. The fifth coalition had been trounced; the British were bottled up in a small part of Portugal behind defensive lines. In 1812 Napoleon's Empire would reach its greatest extent—152 departments embracing 50 million of the 175 million inhabitants of Europe of the time.

Santarem, 1811

Left: "Military survey of Santarem and adjacent country, August 1808. Copy of a reconnaissance by a French officer dated 1801. I delivered a copy of this plan to General Viscount Wellington at Cartaxo on the 6th of January 1811 at which time the head quarters of the French army were at Santarem. This plan appears to be very correct. Signed George Landmann, Captain Royal Engineers."

This document shows Santarem, the location chosen by Massena for his winter headquarters, just a few miles down the Tagus from Lisbon. Having been beaten by Wellington at Busaco and with strong guerilla activity along his extended supply lines, in spring 1811 Massena's Army of Portugal would do exactly what Wellington expected and be forced to move back toward Spain, the army having spent a long hard winter close to starvation.

Right: Map showing lines of Lisbon and military movements around Santarem at the close of 1811. Concentrated in a triangle Santarem–Punhete–Thomar, Massena's three corps (the 2nd in the town of Santarem, Ney's 6th in reserve and the 8th) numbered only some 45,000 effectives by the beginning of December: he had more than 8,000 sick and urgently needed help from Soult's Army of Andalusia.

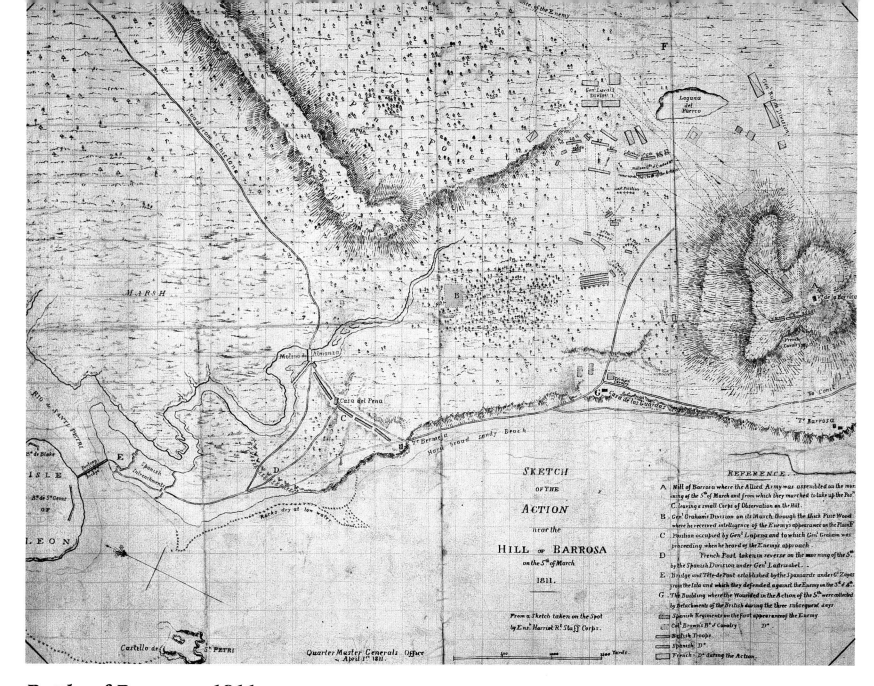

Within the map:

SKETCH
OF THE
ACTION
near the
HILL OF BARROSA
on the 5th of March
1811.

From a Sketch taken on the Spot
by Ens! Harriet R! Staff Corps.

Quarter Master Generals Office
~ April 1st 1811.

500   1000   1500 Yards.

REFERENCE.

A . Hill of Barrosa where the Allied Army was assembled on the morning of the 5th of March and from which they marched to take up the Pos!
C. leaving a small Corps of Observation on the Hill.

B . Gen! Graham's Division on its March through the thick Pine Wood
where he received intelligence of the Enemy's appearance on the Plain F

C   Position occupied by Gen! Lapena and to which Gen! Graham was
proceeding when he heard of the Enemy's approach

D   French Post taken in reverse on the morning of the 5th
by the Spanish Division under Gen! Ladrizabel.

E . Bridge and Tête-de-Pont established by the Spaniards under G! Zayas
from the Isla and which they defended against the Enemy on the 3d & 4th.

G . The Building where the Wounded in the Action of the 5th were collected
by Detachments of the British during the three subsequent days

Spanish Regiments on the first appearance of the Enemy
Col! Brown's B! of Cavalry   D!
British Troops
Spanish D!
French D! during the Action.

Battle of Barrosa, 1811

"Sketch of the action near the hill of Barrosa on the 5th of March 1811 from a sketch taken on the spot by Ensign Harriet of the Regimental Staff Corps." The supreme junta or central assembly of Spain had taken refuge from the French in Cadiz in 1809 and the French had besieged the city. The British commander of the Cadiz garrison was Lt-Gen Thomas Graham (1748–1843), a much-traveled soldier who had seen action in Toulon in 1793, Quiberon Bay in 1795, Italy in 1796, the Mediterranean to 1802, Sweden in 1808, Coruña and Walcheren in 1809. In spring 1811 Graham and Spanish general La Peña planned to land troops from Cadiz behind the besiegers and attack them in the rear. In an expedition plagued by mishaps—including the fact that the Spanish troops ran as soon as they contacted the enemy—Graham and his 5,000 British and Portuguese were forced to take on a numerically superior force of French under General Laval at Barrosa. Graham's tenacity in defense and then timing in the offense saw him carry the day, although with significant casualties, and he was able to regain his position inside Cadiz. The siege would continue until the summer of 1812.

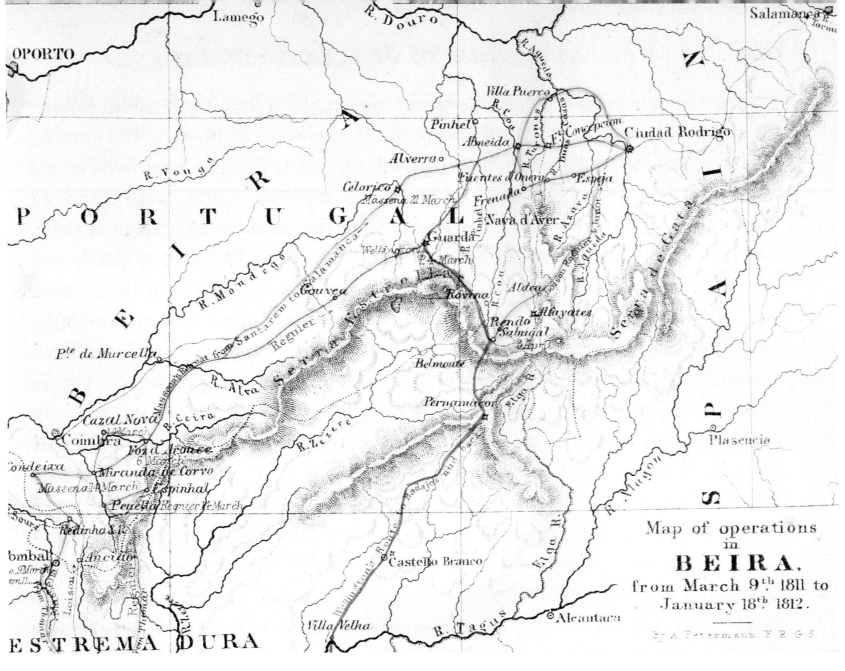

Map of operations
in
BEIRA,
from March 9th 1811 to
January 18th 1812.

By A. Petermann, F.R.G.S.

Operations in Beira, 1811

Massena left Santarem during the second week of March while Wellington was planning to attack him. There followed a series of engagements between the advance guard of Wellington's forces and the rearguard of Massena's, of which three are illustrated here.

Above: General map of the area of operations from 9 March 1811–18 January 1812.

Right: The retreat of the French Army under Massena: three engagements at Pombal (Above Right) and Redinha (Below Right) on 12 March, and Foz d'Aruce (Far Right) on 15 March. The affair at Redinha has been used by some critics of

Wellington to show how a more energetic push against Ney's rearguard operations could have led to a major victory. Sir Charles Oman did not agree and felt that Wellington was forced to await the arrival of sufficient forces to oppose the enemy without suffering a "bloody check" and that Ney's skilful rearguard held on for just the right length of time: "A quarter of an hour's more delay would have been ruin . . ." On 15 March, however, Picton and Erskine's divisions (the 3rd and Light) caught up with Ney and were pressed into action by Wellington. Ney was only able to retrieve the situation "by dint of hard fighting" in an action that saw some 250 French killed for the loss of 70 British.

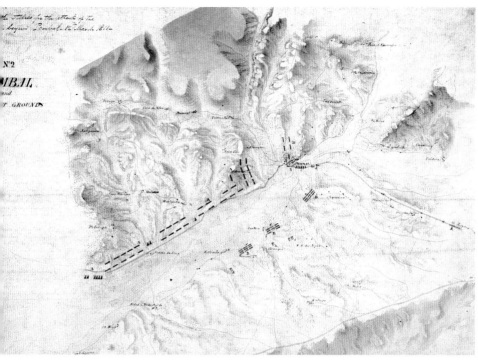

MBAL
and
T GROUND

Nº3

AFFAIR of REDINHA
12ª of March 1811

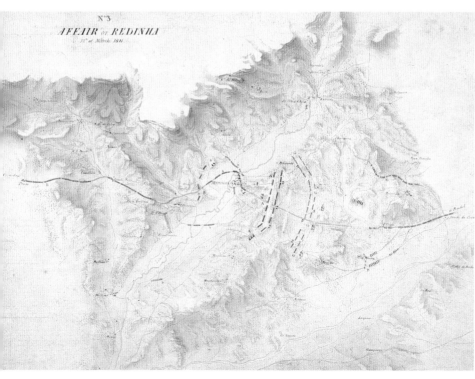

Retreat of Massena Nº VI

POSITIONS
of the
ALLIED and FRENCH ARMIES
On the 12ª of March 1811

Affair at
Foz d'Rouce
15 March 1811

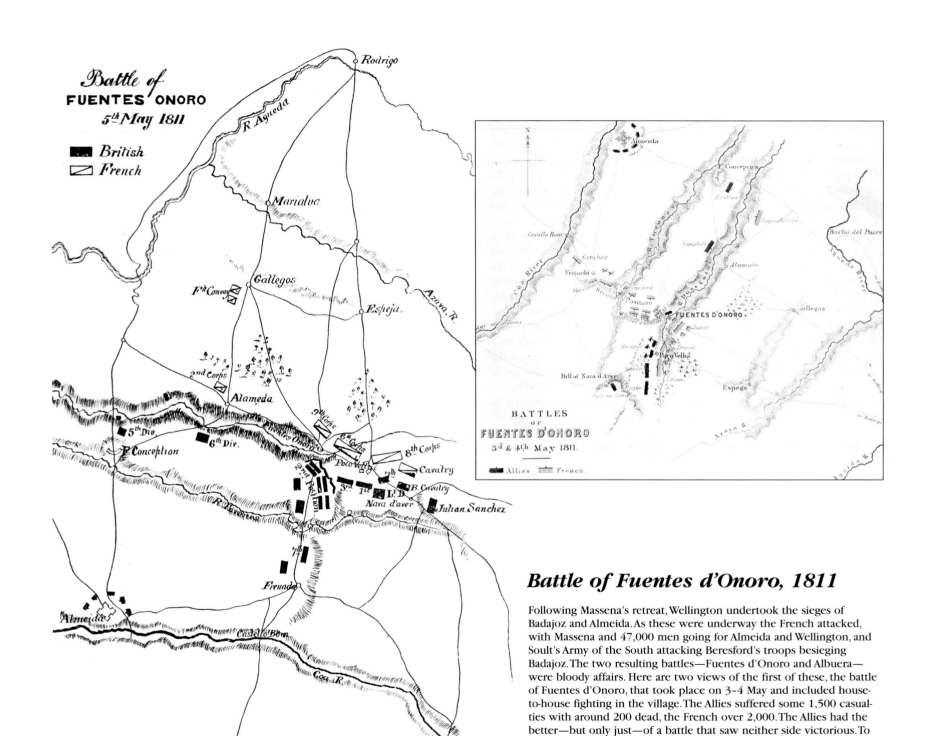

Battle of
FUENTES' ONORO
5ᵗʰ May 1811

British
French

Battle of Fuentes d'Onoro, 1811

Following Massena's retreat, Wellington undertook the sieges of
Badajoz and Almeida. As these were underway the French attacked,
with Massena and 47,000 men going for Almeida and Wellington, and
Soult's Army of the South attacking Beresford's troops besieging
Badajoz. The two resulting battles—Fuentes d'Onoro and Albuera—
were bloody affairs. Here are two views of the first of these, the battle
of Fuentes d'Onoro, that took place on 3–4 May and included house-
to-house fighting in the village. The Allies suffered some 1,500 casualties with around 200 dead, the French over 2,000. The Allies had the
better—but only just—of a battle that saw neither side victorious. To
compound things, most of the French garrison at Almeida under
General Brennier escaped following the town's surrender.

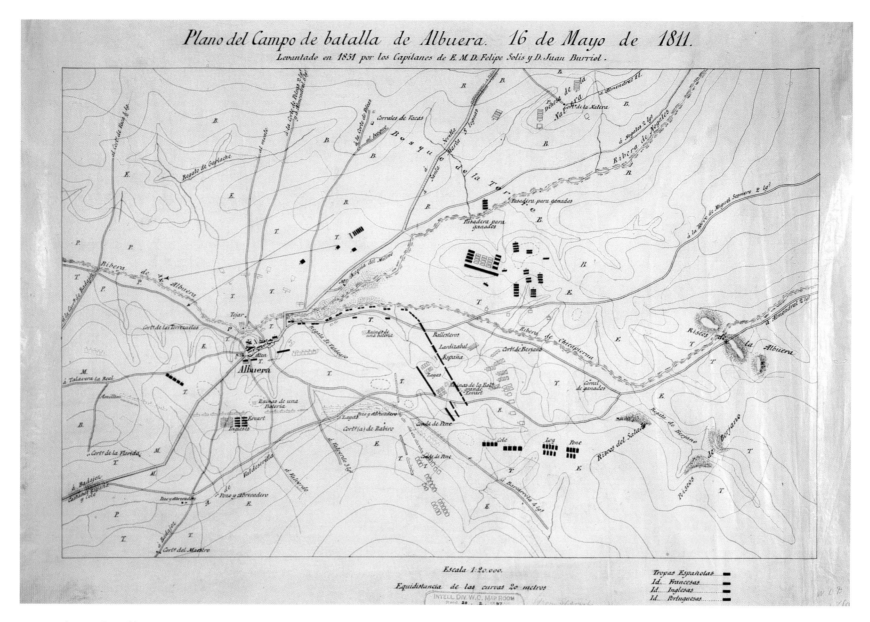

Plano del Campo de batalla de Albuera. 16 de Mayo de 1811.

Levantado en 1851 por los Capitanes de E. M. D. Felipe Solis y D. Juan Burriel.

Escala 1:20.000.

Equidistancia de las curvas 20 metros

Tropas Españolas
Id. Francesas
Id. Inglesas
Id. Portuguesas

Battle of Albuera, 1811

"Plan of the battle of Albuera, 16 May 1811 produced in 1851 by Captains Felipe Solis and D. Juan Burriel."

The battle at Albuera was an even more bloody affair. Left in command of the siege of Badajoz Beresford showed that while he was an administrator without equal, his generalship on the battlefield was not as good, and it was only the tenacity of the British line that defeated the attacks of columns of Soult's Army of the South. There were some 13,000 casualties on the field that day, the bloodiest battle of the Peninsular War it terms of percentages of men committed to the battle, and after Soult had taken the initiative the British victory was down to the attack of the British Fusilier Brigade and defense of its left wing by two untried Portuguese units, the 11th and 23rd. The Fusiliers lost half their men in the attack on a numerically stronger force but carried the day. Unfortunately, however, while Beresford was at Albuera the French had been able to destroy his siege works around Badajoz. When Wellington came to Badajoz to renew the siege he had to retreat back to Portugal in the face of Massena's successor, Marshal Auguste-Frédéric Marmont (1774–1852) who had been ennobled as duc de Ragusa following a five-year period as Governor-General of Dalmatia. Marmont's force combined with Soult to force Wellington westward.

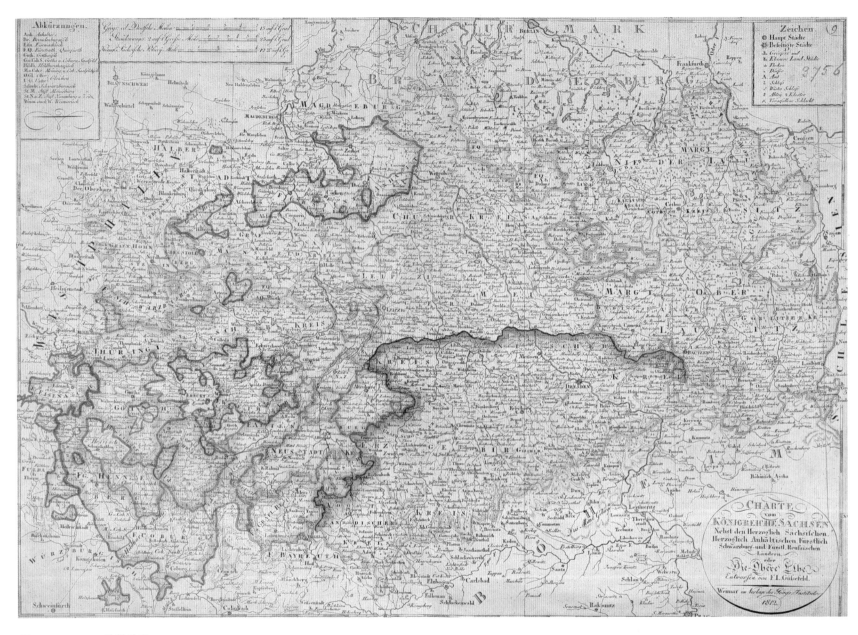

Saxony, 1812

Map of the Electorate of Saxony showing the area from Brunswick and Frankfurt in the north to Schweinfurt in the southwest and Bohemia in the southeast. Saxony, as with so many European states in the period, fought on both sides at one time or another, often depending on the "advice" of their nearest neighbors. Saxony sided with the first and fourth coalitions, mainly because of Prussian pressure, but agreed a neutrality treaty with France in 1796, joined the French-inspired Confederacy of the Rhine in December 1806 (at which time the Elector became King Frederick Augustus I) and sided with Napoleon in his 1809, 1812 and 1813 campaigns. However, at Leipzig (see page 118) Saxon troops changed sides and Frederick Augustus was imprisoned by the Allies. Russia ran the country until the end of 1814 when Prussia took over. At the Congress of Vienna Prussia took over half Saxony's land area, leaving Frederick Augustus as king to rule what remained until his death in 1827. Saxony would never regain its prominence in European politics.

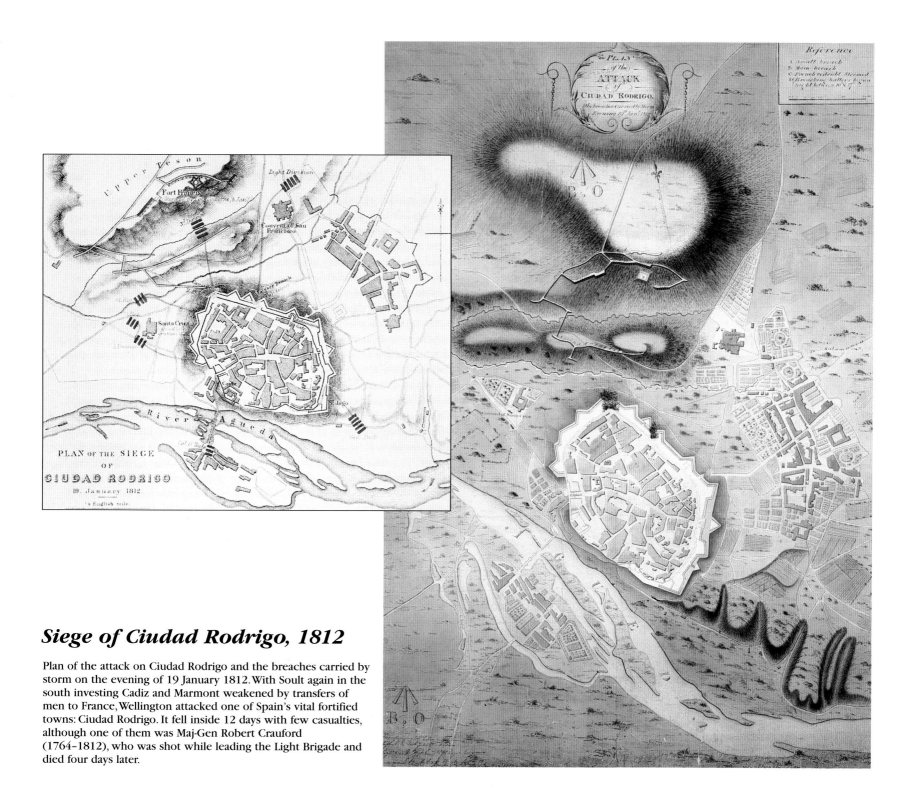

Siege of Ciudad Rodrigo, 1812

Plan of the attack on Ciudad Rodrigo and the breaches carried by
storm on the evening of 19 January 1812. With Soult again in the
south investing Cadiz and Marmont weakened by transfers of
men to France, Wellington attacked one of Spain's vital fortified
towns: Ciudad Rodrigo. It fell inside 12 days with few casualties,
although one of them was Maj-Gen Robert Crauford
(1764–1812), who was shot while leading the Light Brigade and
died four days later.

97

REFERENCES

Fort St Christoval
Tete de Pont
Pardaleras
Ft La Picurina
Ravelin of St Roque
Redoubt from Cœur
Castle
Bn of S Vincent
Bn of S Joseph
Bn of S Jago
Bn of S John
Bn of S Roque
Bn of S Maria
Bn of S Trinadad
Bn of S Peter

Siege of Badajoz, 1812

"Plan of the attack on Badajoz carried on the evening of the 6th of April 1812."
Before the French could react to the fall of Ciudad Rodrigo, Wellington invested
Badajoz for the second time. The siege was not to end as happily as that of
Ciudad Rodrigo. The threat of Soult and Marmont led to an attack before the
defenders had been suitably softened up. Wellington took the city—which his
soldiers then pillaged mercilessly for three days—but at a great cost: more than
5,000 died in the siege, nearly 3,500 of those in the final attack.

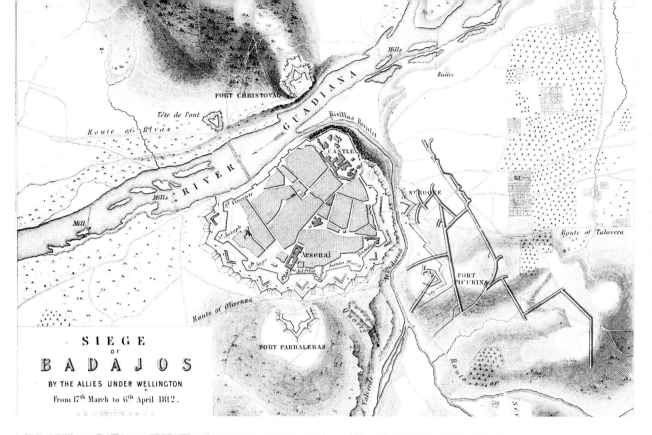

Left: The fall of Badajoz led to a frenzy of plundering and pillaging by the attackers. But not all the stories of Badajoz are of an appalling nature. Sir Charles Oman recounts the story of the rescue of a young Spanish lady by Harry Smith of the 95th. He married Juana de Leon two days later, Wellington giving away the bride, who would become the Lady Smith whose name was given to a South African town that was the scene of another great siege in the Boer War.

Below Left: Map showing location of Badajoz.

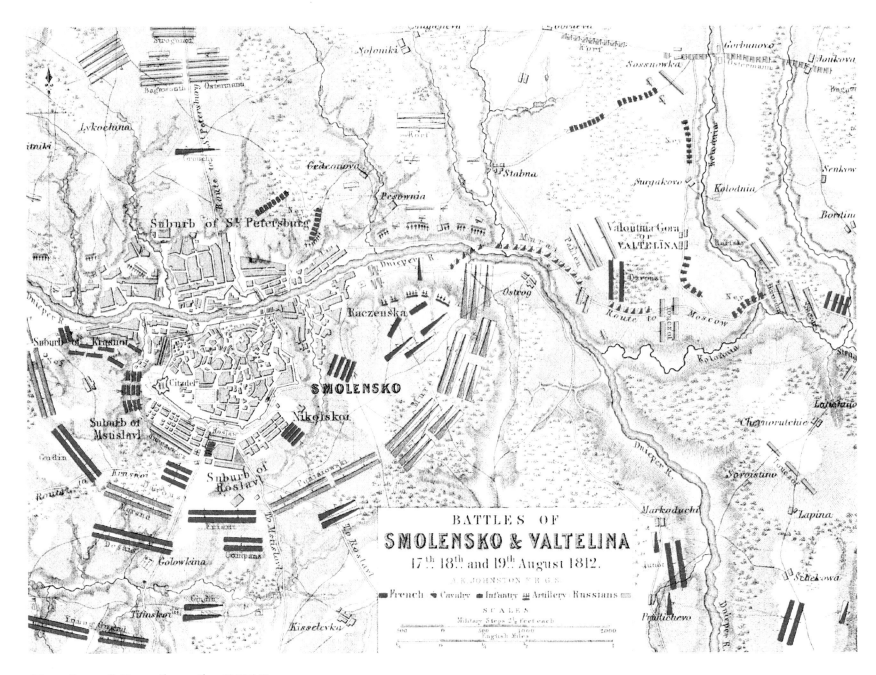

BATTLES OF SMOLENSKO & VALTELINA
17th 18th and 19th August 1812.

A.K.JOHNSTON F.R.G.S.

French ● Cavalry ■ Infantry ▥ Artillery Russians ▬

SCALES
Military Steps 2½ feet each
English Miles

Battle of Smolensk, 1812

One of the reasons why the French forces in Spain proved less capable of resisting Wellington and the Allies in 1812 was Napoleon's invasion of Russia. Up till then he had involved himself in Spanish matters, not letting his brother Joseph have the freedom of command he wished. The attack on Russia took place on 23 June as Napoleon led a 250,000-man army east. In total Napoleon would involve over half a million men in the Russian campaign: fewer than 100,000 would return. By the time of the battle of Smolensk on 16–18 August, he had lost nearly 100,000 men and his handling of the campaign had become strangely hesitant. He could have moved against Smolensk earlier than he did, but waited a day to regroup and, rather than cutting off the Russians' retreat, got bogged down in street fighting. He took the city two days later but the Russian armies had escaped by this time and he had still been unable to bring them to a decisive battle. He decided to head east and try once more, and the stage was set for the major battle of the Russian campaign, Borodino.

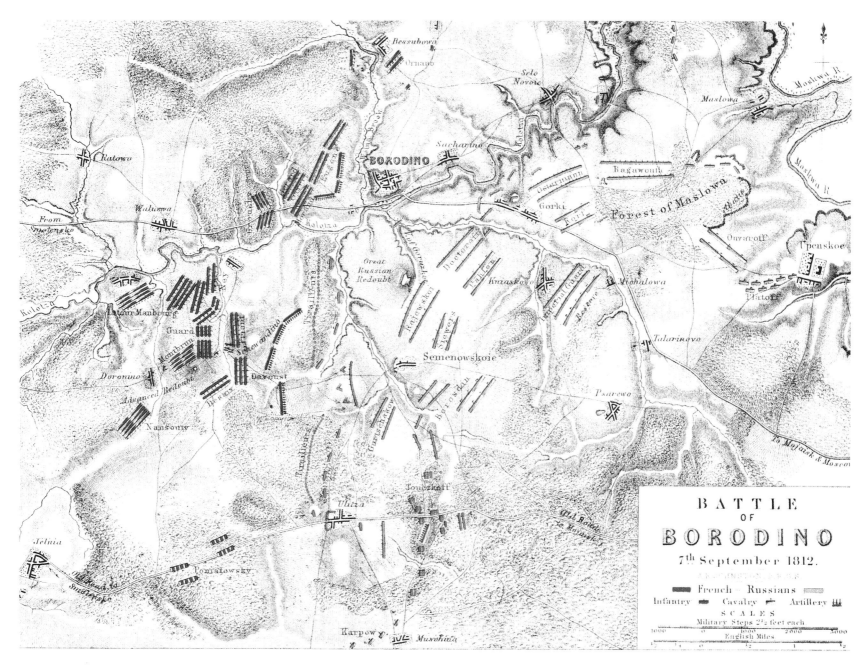

Battle of Borodino, 1812

Fought some 75 miles west of Moscow on 7 September 1812, Borodino was one of the bloodiest Napoleonic battles—one that makes the Peninsular War affairs seem like skirmishes. The French attacked the Russian positions head on and, ultimately, won the day. The moment of the capture of the Raevsky Redoubt was probably the Grande Armée's highest point; the Russians would retire leaving the road to Moscow open. But such was the cost of the battle that Napoleon's forces were down to less than 100,000. It is still difficult to be precise about casualty figures, but Christopher Duffy in his excellent book on Borodino suggests that the Russian casualties were between 38,500 and 44,000, including 23 generals, one of which was General Peter Bagration (1765–1812) who had led the Russian left wing. The French figure is similarly difficult to assess, although it was definitely over 30,000, including Marshal Davout wounded and 47 major- and lieutenant-generals killed or wounded.

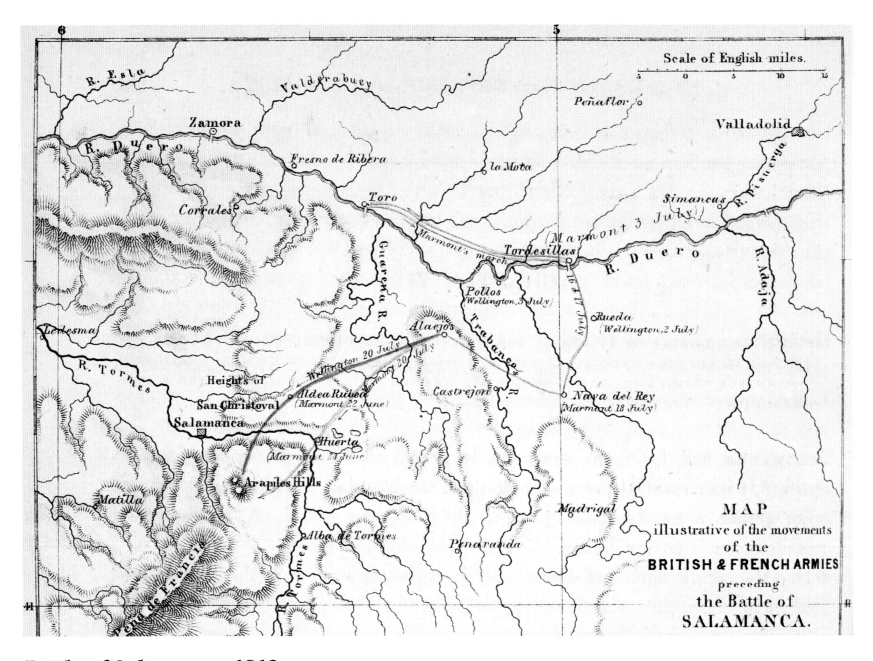

Scale of English miles.

MAP
illustrative of the movements
of the
BRITISH & FRENCH ARMIES
preceding
the Battle of
SALAMANCA.

Battle of Salamanca, 1812

The main battle of 1812 in the Peninsular War was fought south of Salamanca between Wellington's 51,000 men and Marmont's 49,000. By this stage in the campaign Wellington's cipher expert, Major George Scovell (1774-1861), had been able to break the French *Grand Chiffre* (great code) to such an extent that an intercepted message to Marmont from Joseph Bonaparte was sufficiently deciphered to tell Wellington that French reinforcements were on their way. Wellington had to attack—before the 13,000 men of Joseph's army reached Marmont—or be forced once again to retreat. In the end, the battle was decided by a brilliant cavalry charge by the Heavy Brigade and the Allies lost 5,000, as against the French army's 13–14,000.

Above: Map showing area around Salamanca and the battle of 22 July.

Right: Another view of the battle.

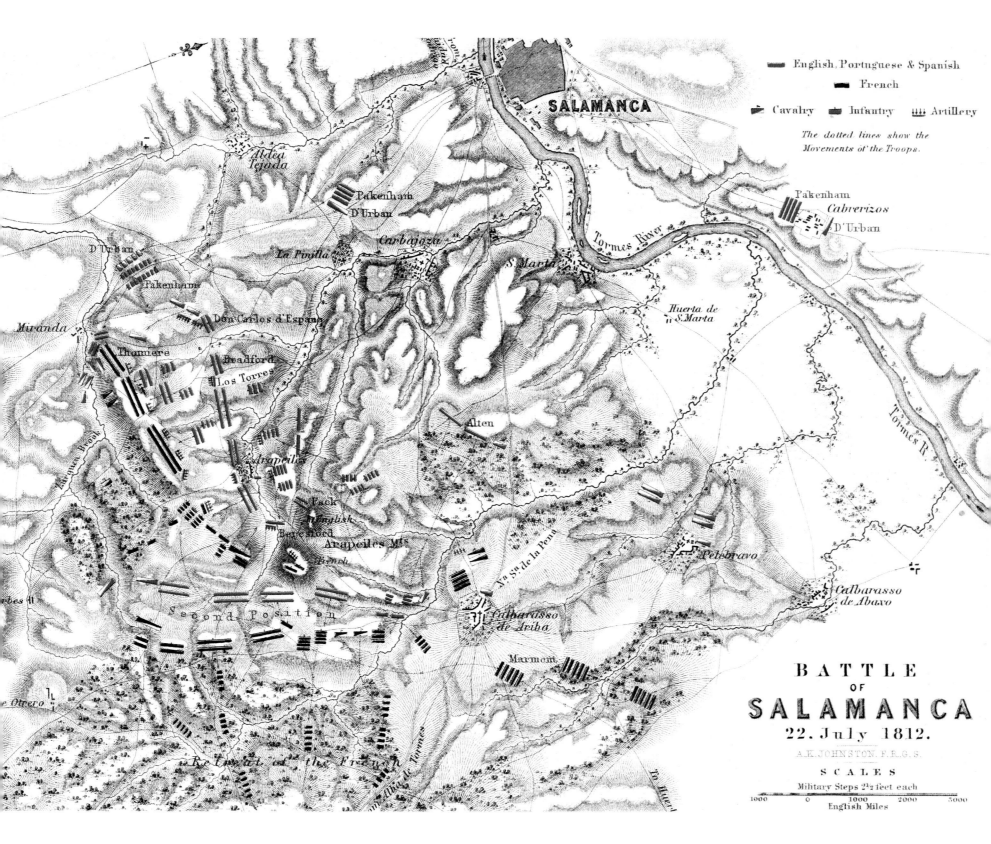

SALAMANCA

English, Portuguese & Spanish
French
Cavalry   Infantry   Artillery

*The dotted lines show the
Movements of the Troops.*

Aldea Tejada

Pakenham
D'Urban

Carbajoza

La Pinilla

D'Urban

Pakenham

Miranda

Thomiere

Don Carlos d'Espana

Bradford
Los Torres

Arapeiles

Pack
English
Beresford
Arapeiles Mts
French

Second Position

Retreat of the French

e Otero

Pakenham   *Calverizos*
D'Urban

Tormes River

S. Marta

Huerta de
S. Marta

Alten

N.ª S.ª de la Pena

Calbarasso
de Ariba

Marmont

Tormes R.

Pelebravo

Calbarasso
de Abaxo

**BATTLE
OF
SALAMANCA
22. July 1812.**

A.K.JOHNSTON, F.R.G.S.

SCALES
Military Steps 2½ feet each

1000   0   1000   2000   5000
English Miles

103

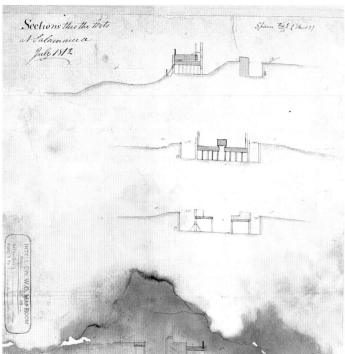

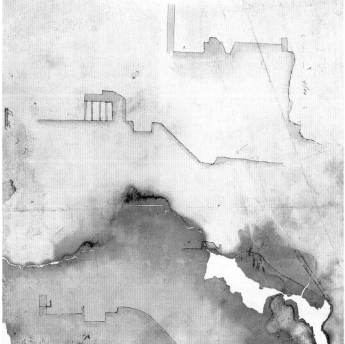

Above: Plan of the attack on the French forts at Salamanca, June 1812.

Above Right and Right: Sections of the forts at Salamanca.

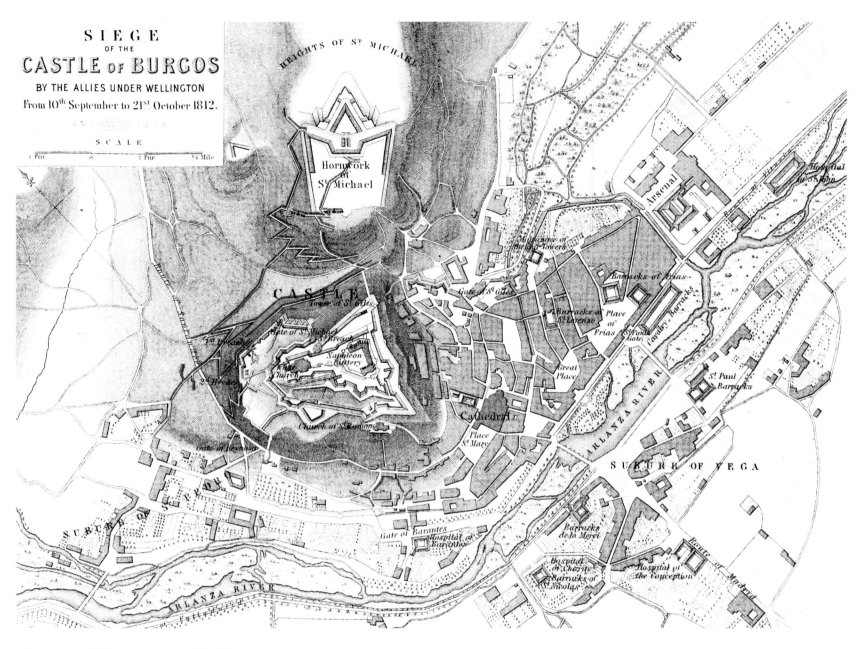

SIEGE
OF THE
CASTLE OF BURGOS
BY THE ALLIES UNDER WELLINGTON
From 10th September to 21st October 1812.

SCALE

Siege of Burgos, 1812

The success at Salamanca may have given the Allies cause for celebration, but the events that followed forced them onto the back foot again. After Salamanca Wellington moved to take Burgos while Hill took a force to liberate Madrid. Burgos was strongly defended as these two plans of the castle show. Initial successes on 19 September saw the Allies take outlying areas, but after a further month of siege Burgos remained intact and Wellington—menaced by Suchet—was forced to retreat, as was Rowland Hill (1772–1842), whose troops in Madrid were threatened by Soult's army. The Allies finally made it back to the safety of winter quarters at Ciudad Rodrigo but not before they had lost 3,000 men.

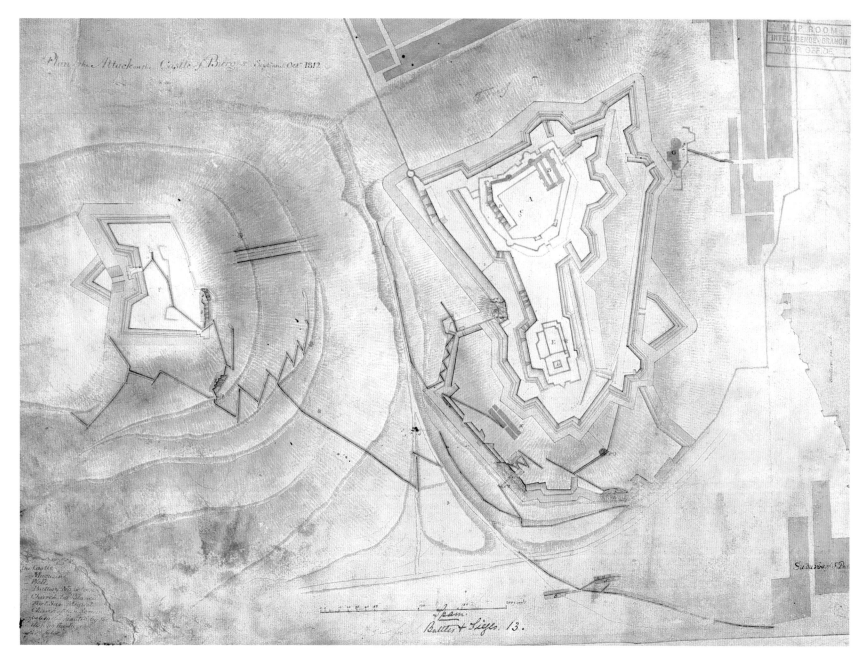

Another view of Burgos.

Key:

A	The castle	E	Church La Blanca
B	Magazine	F	Fort San Miguel
C	Well	G	Fort St Roman
D	Battery Napoleon	z	Palisades planted during the siege

Moscow, 1812

After Borodino Napoleon took Moscow where he waited for Tsar Alexander to sue for peace. He waited a month before he realized that Alexander was going to fight and during this time much of Moscow was destroyed in a fire that many say was started by the Russians themselves. When the French did leave on 23 October, they destroyed parts of the Kremlin, using mines, as is illustrated by this diagram. Luckily, bad weather and the prompt arrival of Russian troops limited the damage.

Key:
1   The high steeple of Ivan Neliki, the cross of which has been taken down, the cupola bent on one side, and pierced through in different places.
2   The Church of St Nicholas, with the steeple on which was hung a great bell weighing 3,500lb blown up by a mine and entirely destroyed.
3   The three cathedrals—of the Assumption, St Michael and the Annunciation—these have been profaned, pillaged and the glasses all broken.
4   The Imperial Palace which was burned when the enemy quitted Moscow and nothing but the walls remain.
5   The arsenal blown up by a mine—more than the half destroyed. The tower in the corner half blown down and cracked in several places, which is likewise the case with the tower on the gate of Nikolski.
6   A tower in the corner of the Kremlin next to the Stone Bridge which was lately rebuilt, sprung and entirely destroyed to the very foundation. It fell across into the river and broke the iron railings along the quay.
7   A tower by the side of the river blown up by a mine to the very foundation.
8   A tower likewise blown down to the very foundation. The iron railing before which have been broken down and thrown into the river.
9   Wooden bridge burned.
10 Shops, which the enemy had begun to demolish, intending to do the same all round the Kremlin in order to put the latter place in a state of defense if they had been able to remain in Moscow during the winter.
11 Troitsky Gate.
12 Monastery called the Resurrection.
13 Archbishop's palace.
14 Monastery of Miracles of the Great Synod.
15 Church of the 12 Apostles.
16 Hall of the Ancient Patriarchs.
17 New building intended for a museum or treasury.
18 The Senate House.
19 Gate of St Nicholas.
20 Gate of the Trinity.
21 The House of the Commandant.
22 Stables.
23 The Church of St Barbe.
24 Gate of Borovsky.
25 Secret Gate.
26 St Nicol.
27 The stone bridge over which the French made their retreat.
28 The great bell sunk into the ground and covered over with rubbish.'

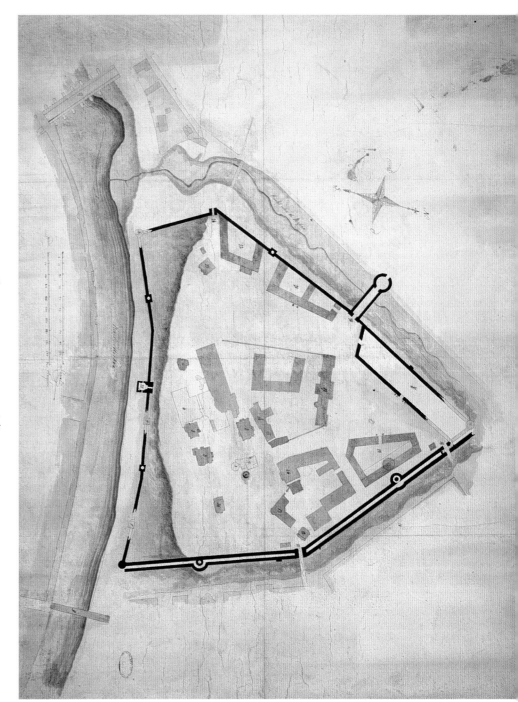

Eastern Europe, 1813

Map showing the Kingdom of Poland, with Prussia to the west and Russia to the east. Moscow is just off the map at upper right. The remnants of Napoleon's shattered Grand Armée made their way back into Poland chased by the Russians who occupied Warsaw early in February 1813. The sixth coalition began to put together armies in the field that they felt sure would be able to topple Napoleon—among them Prussians under Wittgenstein, Yorck and Bülow; Swedes under Crown Prince Bernadotte; and, of course, the Russians under Kutuzov. The scene was set for a campaign that would see French victories but that would end in French defeat. At the Congress of Vienna the great medieval kingdom of Poland was shared out between its neighbors save for a small republic (see page 141).

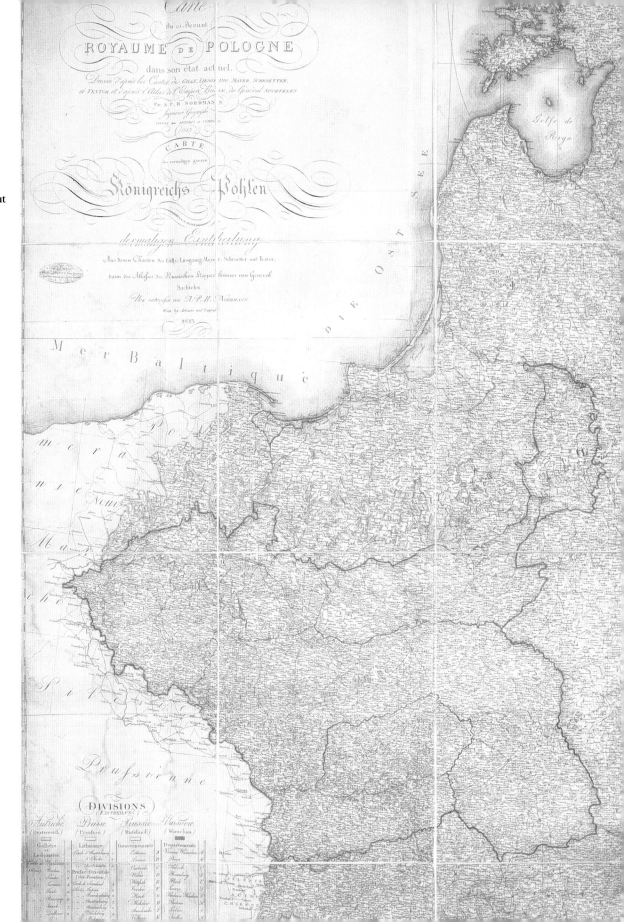

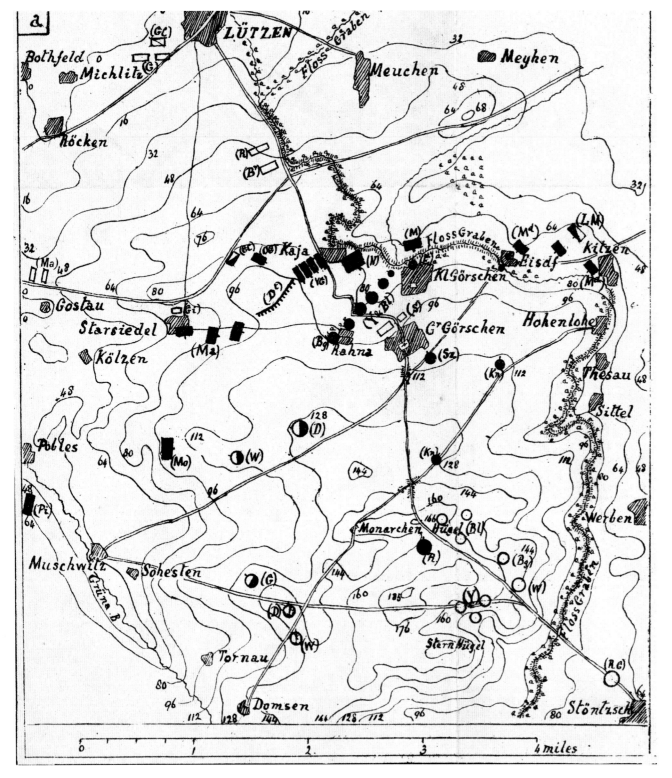

Battle of Lützen, 1813

Following the invasion of Russia, this was the first major battle of the 1813 German campaign. Some 20,000 men on each side were casualties in a battle that started with Wittgenstein's attack on Ney. In spite of assistance from Blücher's and Yorck's corps, Napoleon regained his winning touch after the disasters of the previous year and forced the Allies to retreat. This map shows troop positions about 11:00 in clear; those at 18:00 are shaded. Figures are approximate heights in feet above the contour.

The French

G	Guard Infantry
GC	Guard Cavalry
YG	Young Guard
OG	Old Guard
N	Ney with remains of four divisions, III Corps
Md	Macdonald, XI Corps
LM	Latour-Maubourg 1st Cavalry Corps
R	Richard's Division, III Corps
Br	Brennier's Division, III Corps
M	Marchand's Division, III Corps
S	Souham's Division, III Corps
Gi	Girard's Division, III Corps
Ma	Marmont, VI Corps
Mo	Morand Division, IV Corps
Pi	Pieri's Division, IV Corps
Bt	Brooke's 80-gun battery

The Allies

Bl	Blücher's Corps
Y	Yorck's Corps
Bg	Berg's Corps
E	Prince Eugen of Württemberg
D	Dolff's Prussian Reserve Cavalry
W	Winzingerede's Corps
R	Reserve
RG	Russian Guard and Grenadiers
Kn	Konownitzin's two divisions of Russian Grenadiers
G	Gallitzin—Russian Guard Cavalry
Sz	Steinmetz's Division, Yorck's Corps

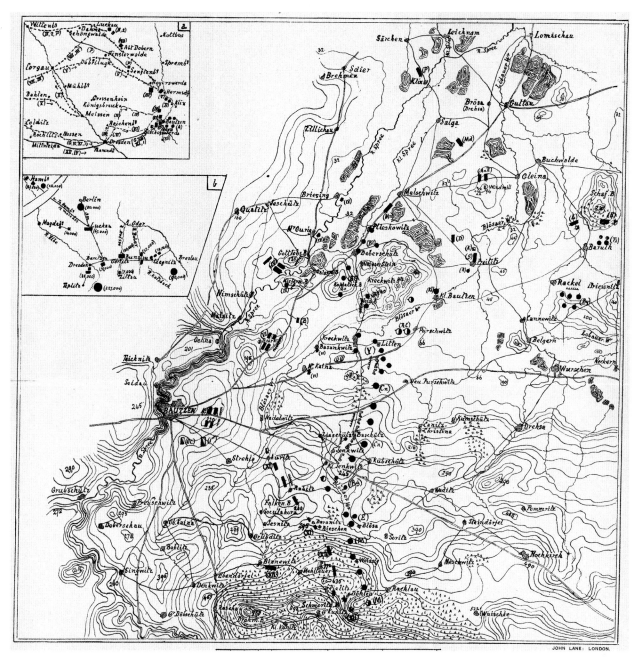

Battle of Bautzen, 1813

After Lützen, the Allied army fell back to Bautzen where Napoleon attacked again. Once more the French were victorious with the casualties some 20,000 on each side, but again Napoleon was left waiting to deliver the knockout blow. The map shows the positions of the armies at about 11:00. Figures are approximate heights in feet above the River Spree.

The French

XII	Oudinet's Corps
XI	Macdonald's Corps
GC	Guard Cavalry
1st	Latour-Maubourg's 1st Cavalry Corps
G	Guard Infantry
VI	Marmont's Corps
B	Two regiments of Barrois's Guard Division
IV	Bertrand's Corps
Mn	Maison's Division, V Corps
P	Puthod's Division, V Corps
Md	Marchand's Division, III Corps
A&R	Albert's & Ricard's Divisions, III Corps
D	Delmas's Division, III Corps
S	Souham's Division, III Corps
K	Kellerman's Advanced Guard
L	Lauriston with Legrange's Division, V Corps
R	Rochambeau's Division, V Corps

The Allies

Tz	Tschaplitz's Advanced Guard.
By	Barclay's Corps
R	Röder's Brigade
Kl	Kleist's Corps
RC	Russian Reserve Cavalry
Bl	Blücher's Corps
Y	Yörck's Corps
Cn	Grand Duke Constantine
Bg	Berg's Corps
E	Eugen of Württemberg
M	Miloradewich

Inset (a)

The French march from Lützen to Bautzen, and positions evening of 19 May. Corps numbers given in Roman figures in brackets in positions and on routes of March.

The French

(1)	1st Cavalry Corps
(2)	2nd Cavalry Corps
P	Puthod's Division, V Corps

The Allies

B	Barclay, followed by Yorck, retreating
A	Main position

Inset (b)

General disposition of forces on both sides, middle of August. The approximate strengths of groups are shown by figures in brackets.

Battle of Vittoria, 1813

As Napoleon slugged it out in Germany, Wellington won the crucial strategic battle of the Peninsular War, forcing the French onto the defensive and causing a new rank to be created in the British Army—field marshal—in order to honor the British general. Following Vittoria, the French realized that they could not return it to rule by King Joseph and retreated to the Pyrenees.

Right: The basin of Vittoria showing the movements of the British Army.

Below right: The battle, 21 June 1813.

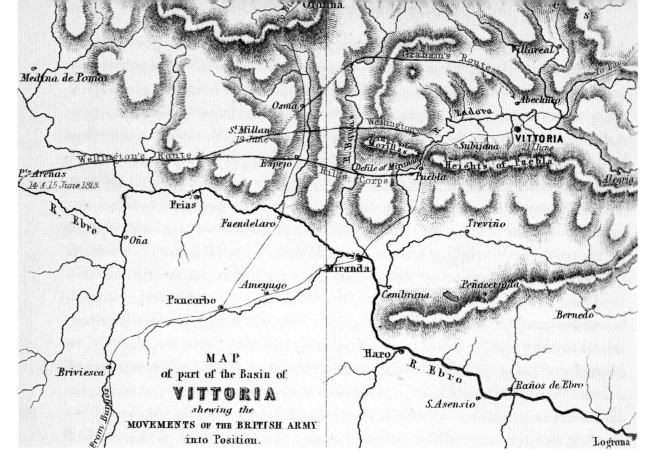

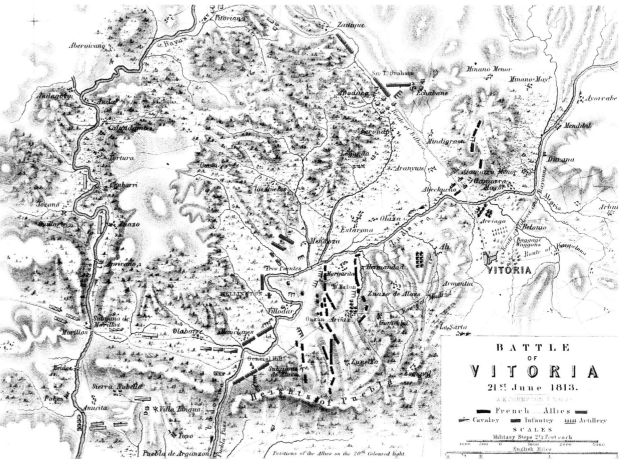

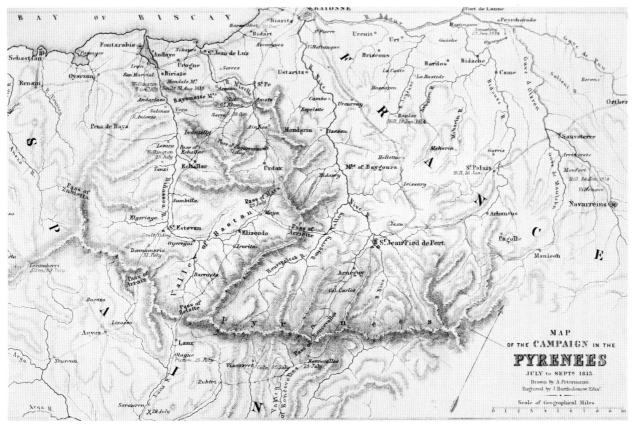

Campaign in the Pyrennes, 1813

Soult took command of the French forces in the area when Joseph Bonaparte returned to Paris. Soult prepared to counter-attack and did so where Wellington didn't expect him— Pamplona rather than San Sebastian, forcing Wellington into a defensive battle at Sorauren on 28 July 1813.

Battle of Sorauren, 1813

The end of Soult's attempt at a counter-offensive, the battle of Sorauren took place after he had won minor victories at Maya and Roncesvalles and had deceived Wellington into thinking his attack would be further north. Wellington raced south when he heard about Soult's advance, and was on hand when he attacked an Allied force composed of 13,000 men under General Sir Galbraith Cole (1772-1842) and 5,000 under Sir Thomas Picton. An additional 6,000 reinforcements arrived just as Soult attacked, and later in the day the arrival of fresh Allied forces under Rowland Hill and General Sir George Ramsay, Earl of Dalhousie (1770-1838), forced Soult to withdraw. He had lost 4,000 men and lost 3,500 more on 30 July; he had lost 13,000 in total by the time he reached France.

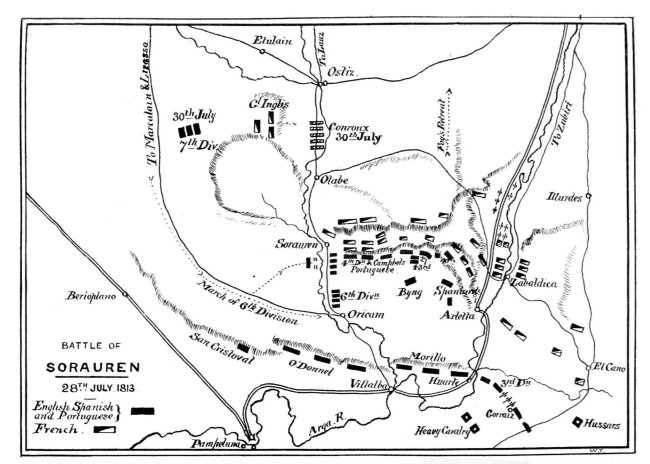

Battle of Gross-Beeren, 1813

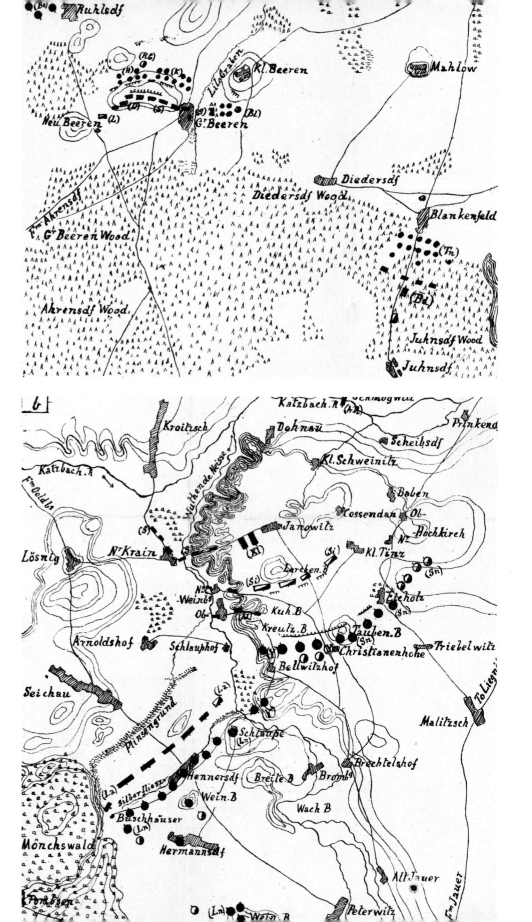

Napoleon's generals did not fare well in August 1813 while the emperor was concentrating on events around Dresden. The Allies planned—by the "Trachenberg Plan"—to avoid battle with the emperor and concentrate on his subordinates. The plan proved remarkably successful. The first of three defeats took place at Gross-Beeren on 23 August when Prussian and Swedish forces defeated General Henri-Gratien Bertrand (1773–1844) and General Jean-Louis Reynier (1771–1814). In the key below, note the commander of the Russian and Swedish troops, Jean-Baptiste Bernadotte, once one of Napoleon's marshals. On 21 August 1810 he had been elected crown prince of Sweden, it is said because he had shown kindness to Swedish prisoners during Napoleon's war with Denmark. Changing his name to Charles-Jean, he had to take control of the country almost immediately because Charles XIII was senile. He would become King Charles XIV in 1818 and the house of Bernadotte rules Sweden to this day. The key below shows the positions of the opposing armies at about 20:30.

The French		The Allies	
S	Saxons of VII Corps	Be	Bernadotte with Russians and Swedes
D	Durutte's Division, VII Corps	H	Hessen-Homburg's Division
L	Lorge's Cavalry	K	Krafft's Division
Bd	Bertrand retiring from Blankenfeld	Bl	Borstell's Corps
		Tn	Tauenzien's Corps at Blankenfeld

Battle on the Katzbach, 1813

The second of three defeats suffered by Napoleon's subordinates while he was active around Dresden, this battle saw Prussian General Gebhard Leberecht von Blücher defeat Marshal Jacques Etienne Macdonald, duke of Tarente (1765–1840) at the River Katzbach on 26 August 1813. The key shows the positions at about 14:00.

The French		The Allies	
Sl	Sebastians's Cavalry	Y	Yorck
XI	Gerard, XI Corps	Sn	Sacken
S	Souham, one division of III Corps	Ln	Langeron
La	Lauriston, V Corps		
AR	Albert's and Ricard's Division, III Corps		

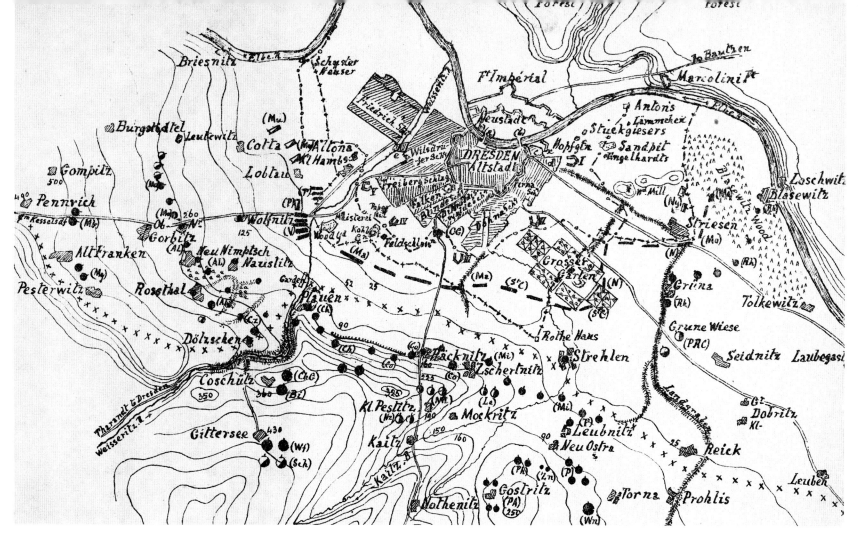

Battle of Dresden, 1813

While his subordinates were being hammered, Napoleon was rushing to the defense of Dresden, where Marshal Laurent Gouvion, Marquis de St Cyr (1764-1830), was attacked on 25 August by over 150,000 troops under Wittgenstein. Napoleon arrived to lead the defense, and later on the 26th received reinforcements that took French strength from 70,000 to 120,000. He won a famous victory, inflicting nearly 40,000 casualties on his enemies, but the defeats of his subordinates rendered his success less significant. The figures on map show approximate heights in feet above level of Altstadt. The troop positions are at the beginning of the battle on 27 August:

Key

I.V.	French redoubts round Altstadt
A	Stone bridge
Bb	Boat and raft bridges
x	Flèche

—o—o—o Extreme limits of Allies advance on 26 August
—+—+—+ French Outpost Line, night of 26 and 27 August
x x x x x French Outpost Line, night of 27 and 28 August

Dresden suburbs not named on map:

c	Ziegel Schlag
d	Rammischer Schlag
e	Lobtau Schlag

The French

Mu	Murat's Cavalry
T	Teste's Division
P	Pajol's Cavalry
V	Victor's Corps (II)
Ma	Marmont's Corps (VI)
OG	Old Guard
StC	St Cyr's Corps (XIV)
N	Ney (Young Guard)
Mo	Mortier (Young Guard)
Ny	Nansouty's Cavalry

The Allies

Rh	Roth's Advanced Guard
PRC	Prussian Reserve Cavalry
Wn	Wittgenstein's Corps
P	Prussians (Kleist etc)
Zn	Ziethen's Advanced Guard
Ph	Pirch's Division
PA	Prince August (Prussian Reserves)
Mi	Miloradowich
ML	Mortiz Lichtenstein's Cavalry
My	Messery's Brigade
Ch	Chasteler's Division
ChG	Chasteler's Grenadiers
Bi	Bianchi's Division
Wf	Weissenwolf's Division
Sch	Schuler's Cavalry
Cz	Czöllich's Brigade
AL	Alois Lichtenstein's Brigade
Mo	Meszko's Division
Mb	Mumb's Brigade

Battle of Kulm, 1813

Right: The third of Napoleon's subordinates to get beaten as part of the Trachenberg Plan, General Dominique Joseph Vandamme (1770-1830) was unlucky enough to get trapped in a Prussian vice. Vandamme and his 32,000 men were supposed to be cutting Allied lines of retreat when they ran into General Ivan Ostermann, Count Tolstoy (1770-1837). While the battle raged, Prussian General Kleist, fleeing Dresden, came up behind Ostermann and trapped the French, causing 11,000 casualties and taking all the others prisoner. The figures on map show approximate heights in feet above sea level. Troop positions at Kulm as at 10:30 as Kleist reached Telinitz.

Key
A—A Original line of French, left and center, in the early morning.
B—B Kleist's line of march, Furstenwald to Nollendorf.
Z   Ziethen's rearguard.
Kl   Kleist's main body.

Siege of San Sebastian, 1813

Below: San Sebastian in northern Spain was besieged between 25 and 31 August 1813, initially by 25,000 men under General Graham (of Barossa fame; see page 91). The port fell on 31 August after heavy Allied casualties—3,700, most in the final assault which was accomplished thanks to the artillery firing over the attackers' heads. The hard struggle led to five days of looting. During the siege, Lt-Col Sir Richard Fletcher, Wellington's incomparable chief engineer and the architect of the Lines of Torres Vedras, was killed.

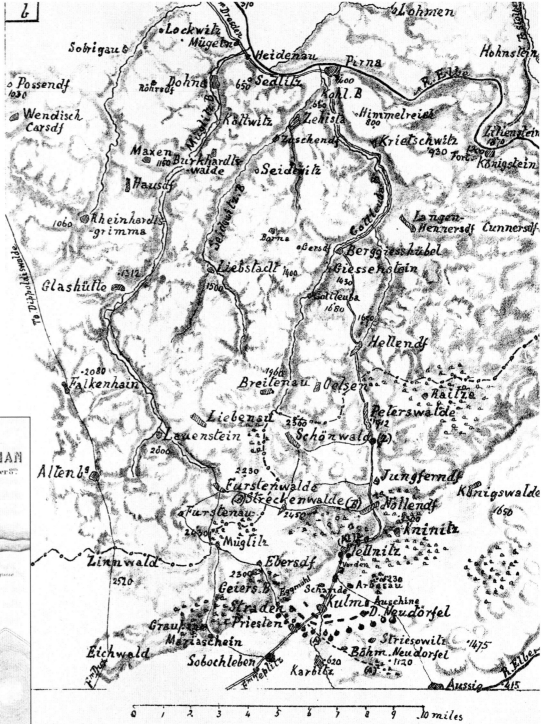

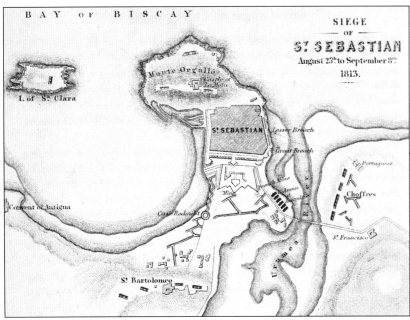

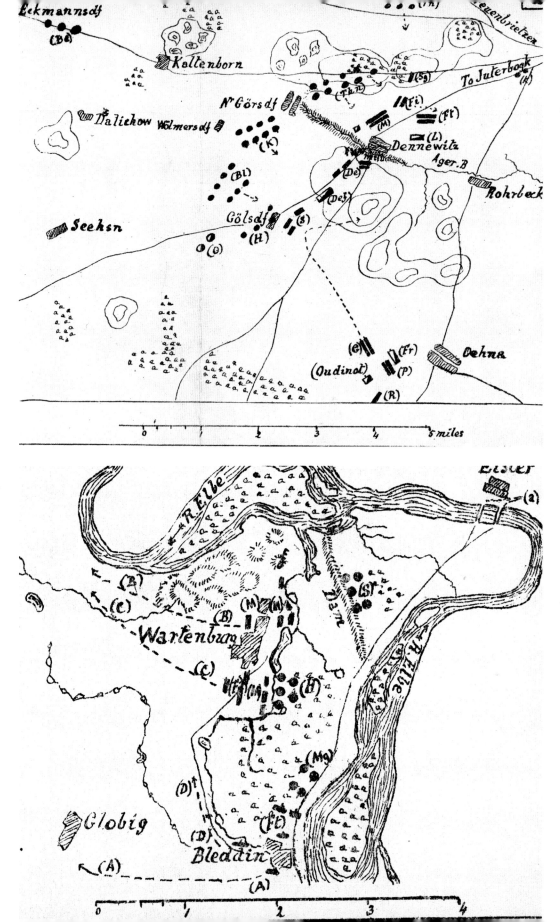

Battle of Dennewitz, 1813

Napoleon sent Ney and 80,000 men toward Berlin but was forced to recall 25,000 men to reinforce Macdonald. In spite of his reduced forces Ney was lured into attacking Bernadotte near Dennewitz and was ambushed by 10,000 Prussians under Bülow. The French suffered high casualties and withdrew to the Elbe. The map shows the positions at around 15:30.

The French		The Allies	
S	Saxons of VII Corps	O	Oppen's Cavalry
Def	Defrance's Cavalry	Bl	Borstell's Corps
De	Durutte's Division, VII Corps	K	Krafft's Division (Bülow's Corps)
M	Morand's Division, IV Corps	H	Hessen-Homburg's Division (Bülow's Corps)
Fl	Fontanelli's Division, IV Corps	Thn	Thümen's Division (Bülow's Corps)
Ft	Franquemont's Division, IV Corps	Tn	Tauenzien's Corps
Sg	Spitzenberg	K	Kleist's Detachment from Juterbogk
G	Guilleminot's Division, XII Corps	Be	Bernadotte with Russians and Swedes
P	Pacthod's Division, XII Corps		
R	Raglowich's Division, XII Corps		
Fr	Fournier's Cavalry		

Battle of Wartenburg, 1813

The passage of the Elbe and action at Wartenburg on 3 October 1813 when Blücher defeated Bertrand and advanced on Leipzig.

The French		The Allies	
M	Morand's Division, IV Corps	S	Steinmetz's Brigade
F	Fontanelli's Division, IV Corps	H	Horn's and Hunerbein's Brigade
Fr	Franquemont's Division, IV Corps	Mg	Prince Charles of Mecklenburg's Advanced Guard
A—A	Line of Franquemont's retreat.	D—D	Prince Charles's move to turn Wartenburg
B—B	Line of Morand's retreat.	a	Prussian bridges over the Elbe
C—C	Line of Fontanelli's retreat.		

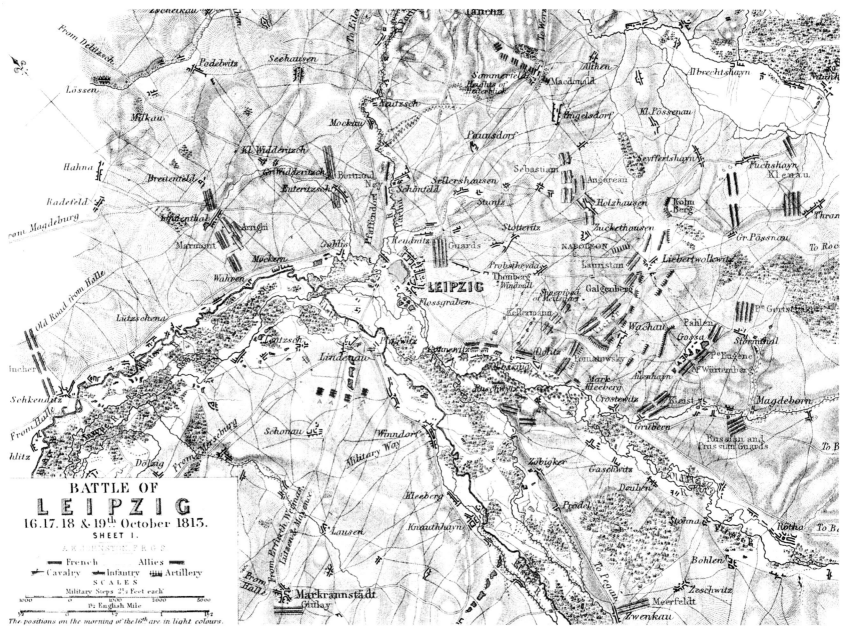

Battle of Leipzig, 1813

Above and Right: The critical battle of the 1813 German campaign was Napoleon's defense of Leipzig on 16–19 October. Second only to Borodino in size of battle, Napoleon's troops were attacked by Bernadotte's Army of the North, Bennigsen's Army of Poland, Schwarzenberg's Army of Bohemia, and Blücher's Army of Silesia. The French Army escaped encirclement during the "Battle of the Nations" and retreated back toward France. Two sheets show the battle. The second sheet includes a plan of the city of Leipzig. Britain's contribution to the "Battle of the Nations" was a rocket troop commanded by Captain Richard Bogue who died in the battle.

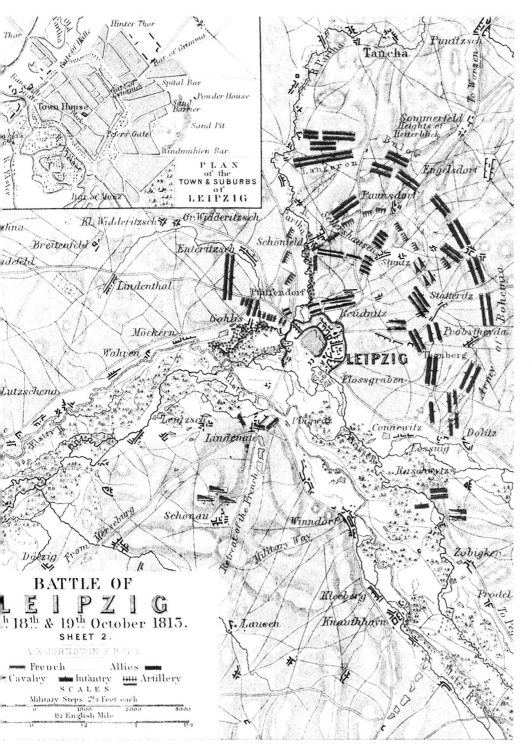

BATTLE OF
LEIPZIG
th 18th & 19th October 1813.
SHEET 2.
A K JOHNSTON F R G S

—— French   —— Allies
Cavalry   Infantry   Artillery
S C A L E S
Military Steps 2½ Feet each

Battle of Hanau, 1813

Napoleon's German allies had started to switch sides even before the battle of Leipzig confirmed Napoleon's loss of control: Bavaria, his main ally, had left the Confederation of the Rhine on 8 October; the Saxons changed sides during the battle. To add insult to injury, the Bavarians attacked the Grand Armée as it retreated; Napoleon had enough strength to defeat General von Wrede at Hanau on 30–31 October.

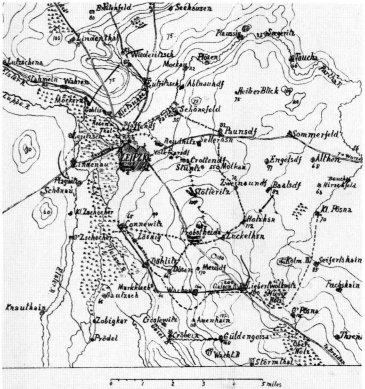

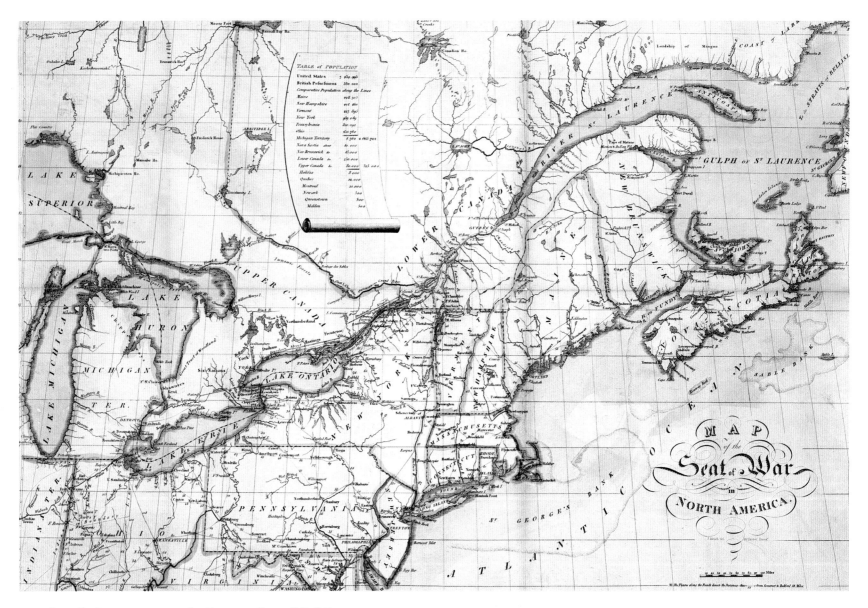

TABLE of POPULATION

United States	7,239,995	
British Possessions	530,000	
Comparative Population along the Lines		
Maine	228,705	
New Hampshire	211,860	
Vermont	217,895	
New York	959,049	
Pennsylvania	810,091	
Ohio	230,760	
Michigan Territory	4,762	4,663,742
Nova Scotia about	40,000	
New Brunswick do.	45,000	
Lower Canada do.	350,000	
Upper Canada do.	80,000	345,000
Halifax	8,000	
Quebec	18,000	
Montreal	10,000	
Newark	500	
Queenstown	500	
Malden	500	

MAP of the Seat of War in NORTH AMERICA.

United States and Canada, 1813

Map of the seat of war in North America Including a key showing populations (USA 7,239,995; British possessions 530,000) by John Melish. In 1812, while the Royal Navy was blockading Napoleon's Europe, Great Britain and the United States fought a three-year war that culminated in a British disaster at New Orleans (see page 123). The friction that had existed between Britain and the United States since the end of the last century, allied to the heavy-handedness of the British blockade—including the attack on the USS *Chesapeake* in 1807— and the thought by some in the United States that they may be able to win more possessions from British Canada, finally caused war. It wasn't a big one, with actions on the Great Lakes and some small land engagements. Toronto (then called York) was captured and burned in 1813 and Washington (including the White House) was burned by the British in 1814. Peace eventually came—but too late for 2,000 redcoats including many Peninsular War veterans and their commander General Edward Pakenham, who lost their lives on 8 January 1815 outside New Orleans.

Southern United States, 1813

Another map by John Melish, this one of the southern sections of the United States including Florida and the Bahama Islands showing the seat of war in that department. A statistical table gives the areas of the states and their population. John Melish (1771–1822) was born in Scotland and settled in the United States in 1811 after visiting the country a number of times. In 1812 he produced the important *Travels in the United States of America*, illustrated with many of his own maps, thus beginning a career as a cartographer and publisher that would see him become one of the most significant of all early U.S. cartographers. After

the commercial success of the general map on the Seat of the War (see page 120) that he produced in 1813, Melish went on to produce a number of other maps of regions involved in the war. He would issue them eventually as the *Military and Topographical Atlas*.

Eastern United States, 1813

Map by John Melish of the American Coast from Lynhaven Bay to Narraganset Bay including a key to the populations of the principal cities and towns along from Eastern seaboard from Newport, Connecticut to Norfolk. Note the populations of New York 96,373, Philadelphia 111,210 and Baltimore 35,583, the three most populated cities.

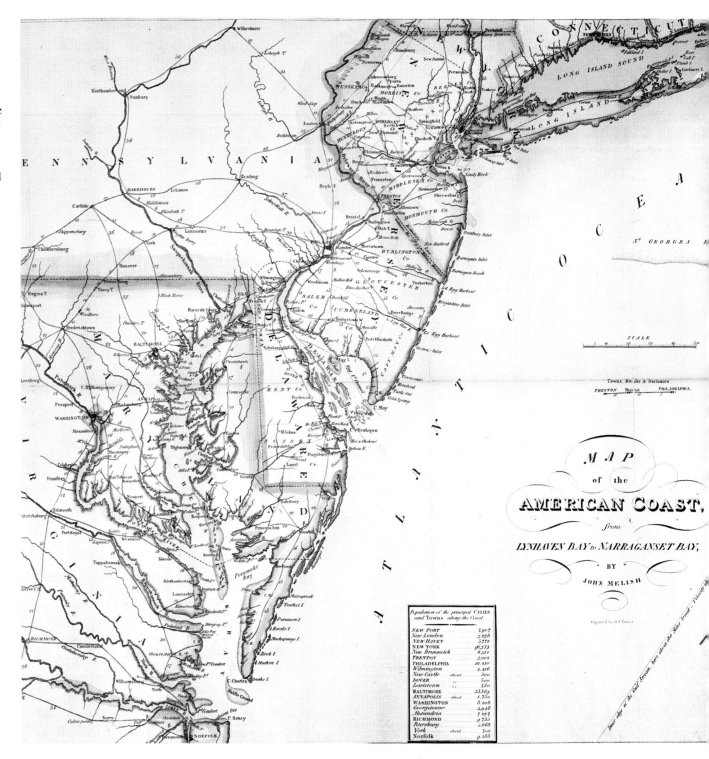

New Orleans, 1815

Map of New Orleans and adjacent country by John Melish, dated 1815.
Note defensive batteries on the Mississippi, Fort St Philip at its mouth and Fort St
John above the city. Under General (later president) Andrew Jackson
(1767–1845) United States' forces first campaigned against Creek indians in the
area of Nashville, then invaded Spanish Florida and took Pensacola, and finally
relieved New Orleans where he gave Pakenham's forces a beating.

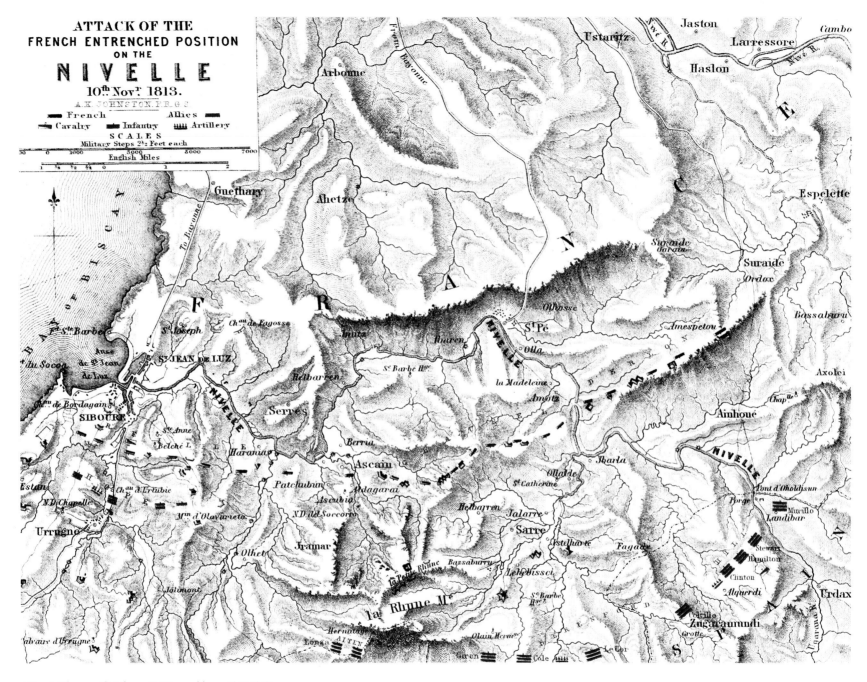

Battle of the Nivelle, 1813

In the southwest, Wellington had crossed the Pyrennes and his army now stood on the threshold of France, tying up large numbers of troops that Napoleon could have used to good purpose in Germany. On 10 November he struck at Soult's forces on the Nivelle River. With 82,000 men, 36,000 of whom were led by Beresford and around a third of whom were green Spanish troops, Wellington again won a victory that would see Soult barely getting his troops into relative safety across the Nivelle after losing nearly 4,500 men and 70 guns.

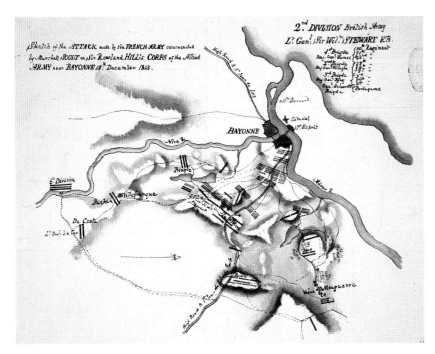

Battles in front of Bayonne, 1813

Left: Sketch of the attack made by the French Army commanded by Marshal Soult on Sir Rowland Hill's Corps of the Allied Army near Bayonne, 13 December 1813. In the thick of the fighting was Lt-Gen Sir William Stewart, KB who commanded the 2nd Division. Key top right identifies the constituents of the division as being: 1st Brigade under Maj-Gen Barnes (50th, 71st and 92nd Regiments); 2nd Brigade under Maj-Gen Pringle (2?, 34, 39); and 3rd Brigade under Maj-Gen Byng (3rd, 517th, 31st); and General Ashworth's Brigade (Portuguese).

Bayonne was invested from 26 February 1814. When Napoleon fell the commander of the garrison, General Pierre Thouvenot (1757–1857), took advantage of the relaxation of the Allied troops to sortie out of the city on 14 April. In a pointless action that saw nearly 2,000 casualties, the British besiegers under General John Hope (1765–1823) pushed the French back. Bayonne would finally surrender on 26 April.

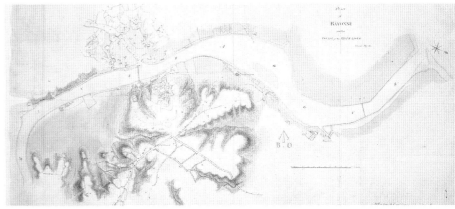

Bayonne and the River Adour, 1814

Right: Plan of Bayonne from 1814 and the bridge of boats thrown across the Adour by FM the Marquis of Wellington on 26 February 1814.

This sort of logistical effort is required by every army. In the British Army, the Peninsular War saw an increase in the numbers and proficiency of engineers, culminating in the creation in 1812 of the Royal Military Artificers or Sappers and Miners (shortened to Royal Sappers and Miners in 1813) who would be trained at Chatham and organized into companies with Royal Engineers' officers. The effects were immediate, and by the Waterloo campaign each division had a Sapper company. The bridge over the Adour was the work of Robert Henry Sturgeon, nephew of the Marquess of Rockingham and an excellent technician.

BATTLE
OF
ORTHEZ
27th January 1814.

BATTLE OF
ORTHES
27th February 1814.
A.K.JOHNSTON,F.R.G.S.
Allies   French
Cavalry   Infantry   Artillery
Positions before and after the Battle, coloured light
SCALES
Military Steps 2½ feet each
English Mile.

English
French

Battle of Orthez, 1814

Across the Adour, with Soult having sent men to answer Napoleon's call for troops in northern France, Wellington attacked the French at Orthez on 27 February. Soult lost 4,000 men after a hard fight and withdrew to the northeast where his forces escaped encirclement at Tarbes only to be attacked again outside Toulouse.

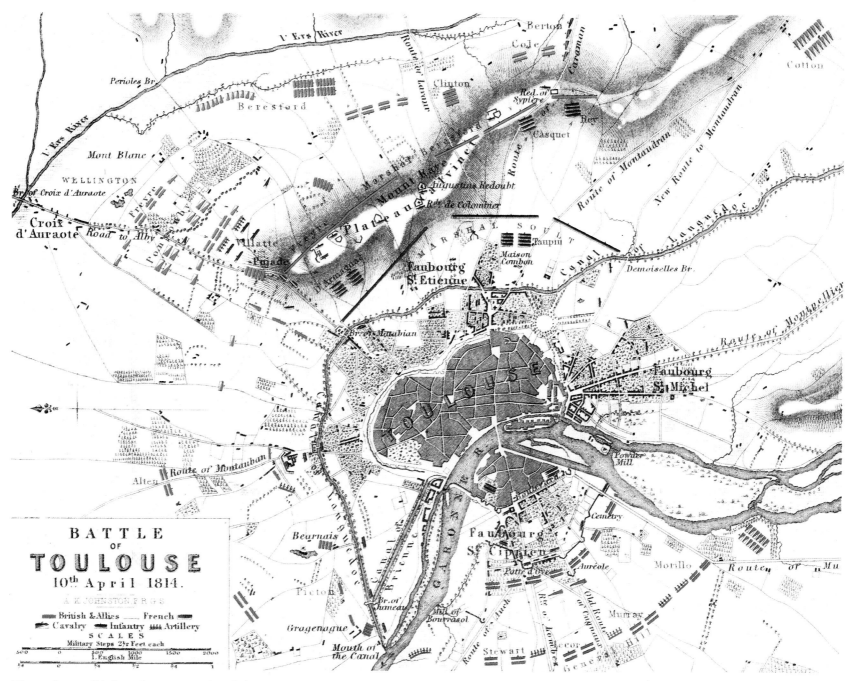

The following labels appear on the map:

BATTLE OF TOULOUSE 10th April 1814.

A.K.JOHNSTON F.R.G.S

British & Allies — French
Cavalry — Infantry — Artillery

SCALES
Military Steps 2½ Feet each
1 English Mile

Battle of Toulouse, 1814

The last major battle of the Peninsular War took place on 10 April. Soult was hammered outside the city, took refuge behind the walls and then gave up the city on the night of 11–12 April, making for Carcassonne. Wellington lost 4,500 men in this final battle and the two armies must have been relieved to hear of Napoleon's abdication (which took place on 6 April) and the end of the war.

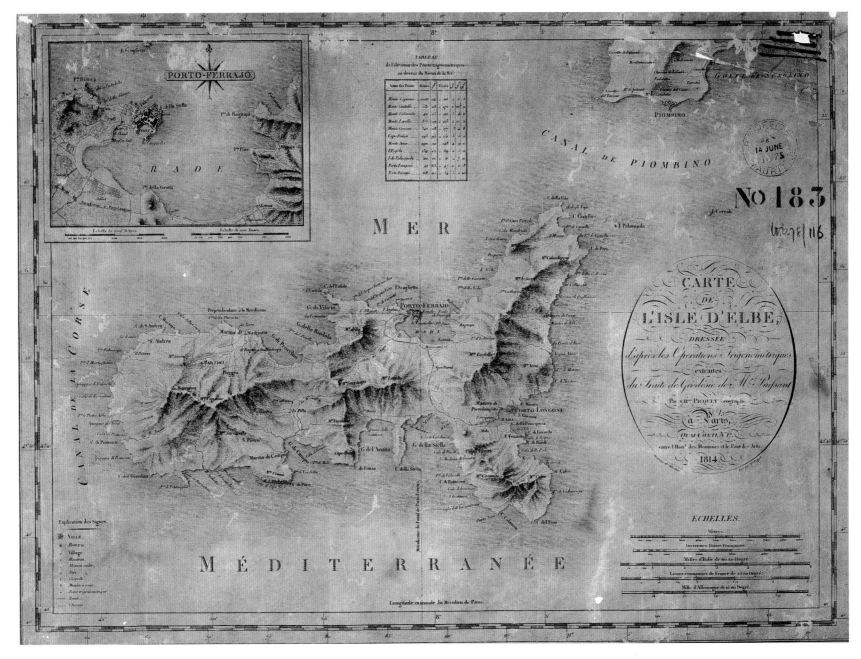

Elba, 1814

French map of the island of Elba with a detail of Porto Ferrajo. Napoleon, after a failed suicide attempt on 12 April, became emperor of this small Mediterranean island on 16 April by the Treaty of Fontainebleau. He arrived on 4 May and it was from Elba that he watched events on the mainland before escaping in February 1815 for his last throw.

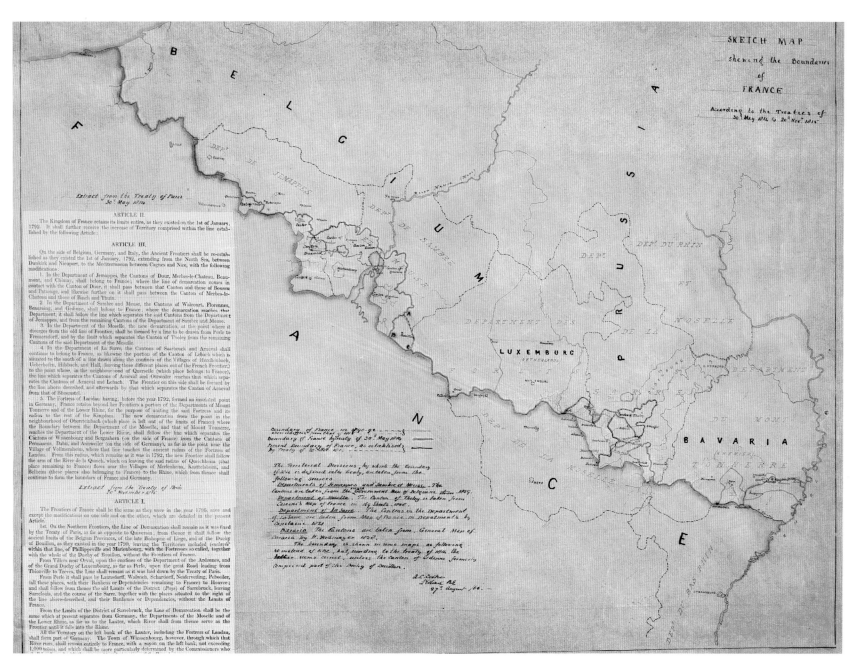

Treaty of Paris, 1814

This is north France from the Channel to Strassburg (Strasbourg). Extracts from the two treaties (30 May 1814 and 20 November 1815) at left. Yellow delineates the 1792 border; green the border agreed in 1814. The most important element to this is that the bulk of the new departments created by Napoleon were returned to their rightful owners.

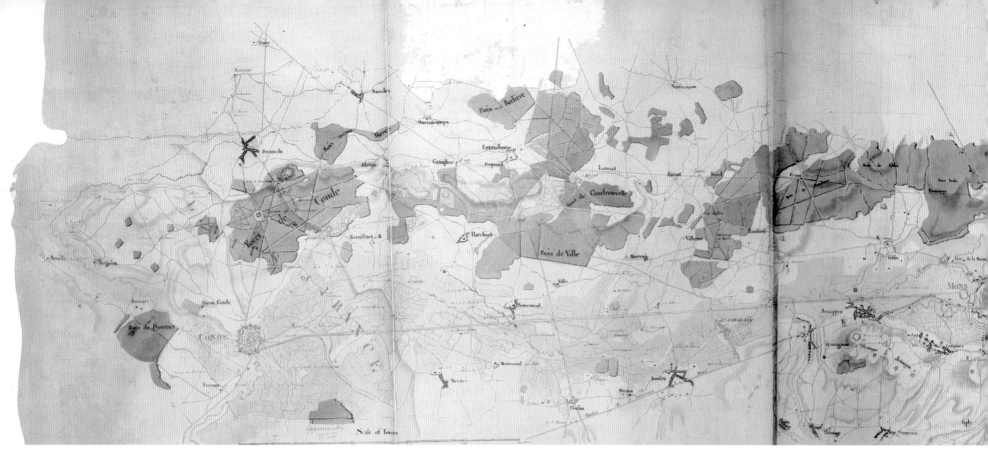

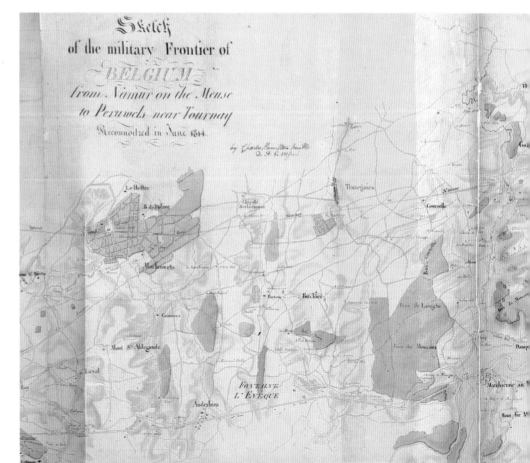

Sketch
of the military Frontier of
BELGIUM
from Namur on the Meuse
to Peruwels near Tournay
Reconnoitred in June 1814.

by Charles Hamilton Smith
Q.M.G. Dep.t

130

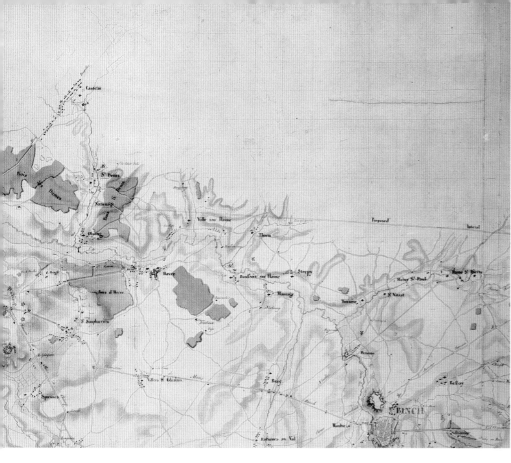

Belgian frontier, 1814

These maps show "A sketch of the military frontier of Belgium from Namur on the Meuse to Peruwels near Tournay. Reconnoitred in June 1814 by Charles Hamilton Smith, Deputy Assistant Quartermaster General." Smith was born in Flanders of a protestant family and served in the 8th Light Dragoons as a volunteer from 1794. Commissioned lieutenant in 1797, he went on to serve in the West Indies and as deputy quartermaster general on the ill-fated Walcheren expedition of 1809 (see page 84). He served in the Netherlands in 1813–14 and in 1816 undertook an intelligence mission in North America. At the time that Smith drew these maps, Napoleon was still on Elba. However, he would return to take on the Allies just a few miles to the north of the area depicted here.

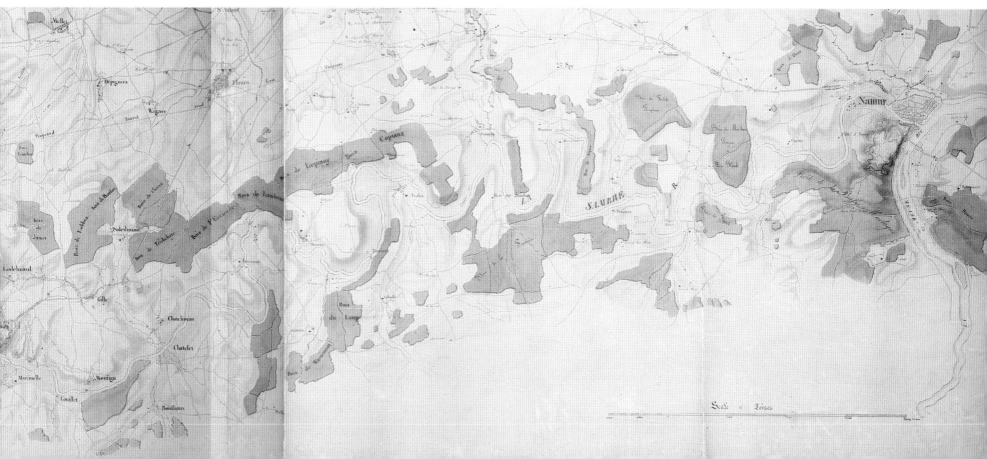

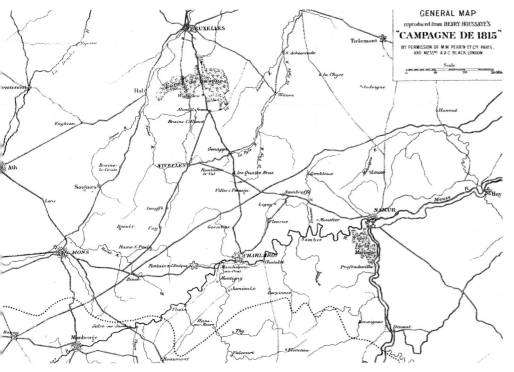

GENERAL MAP
reproduced from HENRY HOUSSAYE'S
"CAMPAGNE DE 1815"
BY PERMISSION OF M.M. PERRIN ET C.º PARIS,
AND MESS.ºˢ A & C BLACK, LONDON.
Scale

Campaign of 1815

The Hundred Days—Napoleon's attempt to turn the clock back and defeat the Allies in 1815—started when he sailed from Porto Ferrajo on Elba (see page 128) on 26 February 1815 and finished in July when he set sail as a captive for St Helena. Between those dates he had, once again, become emperor of France, scared to death the Allies that formed the seventh coalition against him with his brilliant maneuvering and, once again, lost his throne. It was the stuff of legends, and added immeasurably to the mystique of the little Corsican. He landed in France on 1 March with around a thousand men and three generals—Bertrand, Drouot and Cambronne. By the time he reached Paris he had been fêted as a returning hero and the king (Louis XVIII) had fled to Ghent.

French mobilization followed the setting up of the seventh coalition on 25 March—soon Napoleon had nearly 300,000 men at his disposal with nearly 200,000 in training. The Allies planned to raise 650,000, and Napoleon determined that he would strike while these forces were uncoordinated. He secretly assembled his troops in northern France, at Beaumont, in June planning to go for the two strongest opponents—Wellington and Blücher—first. The Armée du Nord would be of 128,000 men, while smaller armies under General Rapp (23,000 men in the vicinity of Strasbourg), General Lecourbe (8,400 in the Jura), Marshal Suchet (23,500 men of the Armée des Alpes), Generals Clausel and Decaen (6,800 and 7,600 men respectively along the Pyrennes) and Marshal Brun (5,500 men on the Riviera) would hold off other Allied armies. A further 60,000 men were in garrisons or under General Lamarque around the Loire Valley. The stage was set for Napoleon's last campaign.

Battle of Quatre Bras, 1815

Wellington was headquartered at Brussels and Blücher at Namur when Napoleon reached Beaumont on 14 June. Napoleon's plan was to separate them and knock them out individually—and the first part of the plan worked brilliantly when Wellington, fearing the French were heading for the Channel ports, moved his troops south and west of Brussels. As Wellington would say when he found out Napoleon's true intentions, "Napoleon has humbugged me . . . he has gained 24 hours' march on me." When asked what he intended to do, Wellington replied, prophetically, "I have ordered the army to concentrate at Quatre Bras; but we shall not stop him there, and if so, I must fight him here." And he pointed to Waterloo.

The second part of Napoleon's plan, pushing the Prussians back, had worked too, as Lt-Gen Hans Ziethen, commander of the Prussian Army's I Corps, had fallen back toward Fleurus when attacked. With Ney advancing into the gap, Napoleon's strategic plan had fallen into place. After detailed reconnaissance he decided to attack Blücher first at Ligny and then Wellington on the 17th. Ney should have attacked at Quatre Bras—a strategic crossroads on the road to Brussels—and, once he had beaten off the enemy, turned right to encircle the Prussians. But, inexplicably, Ney did not advance on the morning of the 16th. It was well into the afternoon before he did so, by which time the Allies had been able to move troops forward. Now Ney's 25,000 men were engaging the Allies' 21,000 and Ney could not play a part at Ligny. Further Allied reinforcements would take that figure to 26,000 and Ney was hard pressed not just to take Quatre Bras, but to withstand the Allies' reconcentrated army.

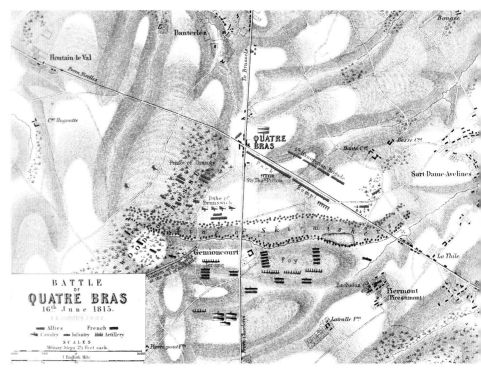

BATTLE
OF
QUATRE BRAS
16ᵗʰ June 1815.

Allies ▬▬▬ French ▬▬▬
Cavalry ▬▬ Infantry ▬▬ Artillery ▬▬▬
SCALES
Military Steps 2½ Feet each.
1 English Mile

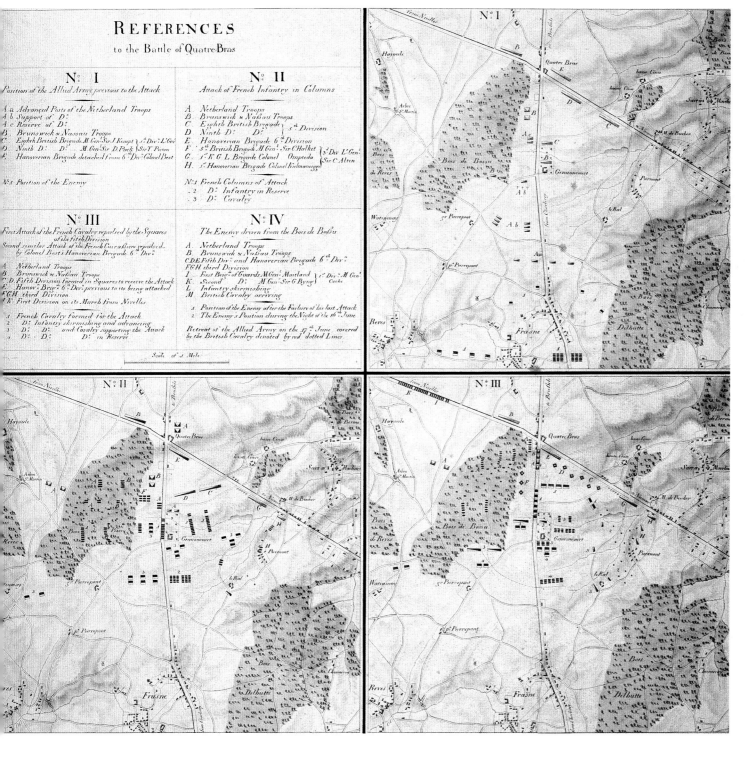

Battle of Quatre Bras, 1815

The battle of 16 June showing:

I   The position of the Allies before the attack.

II   The attack of French infantry in columns.

III   The French cavalry attack repulsed by the 3rd Division's squares and the French cuirassiers' attacks repulsed by Colonel Best's Hanoverians.

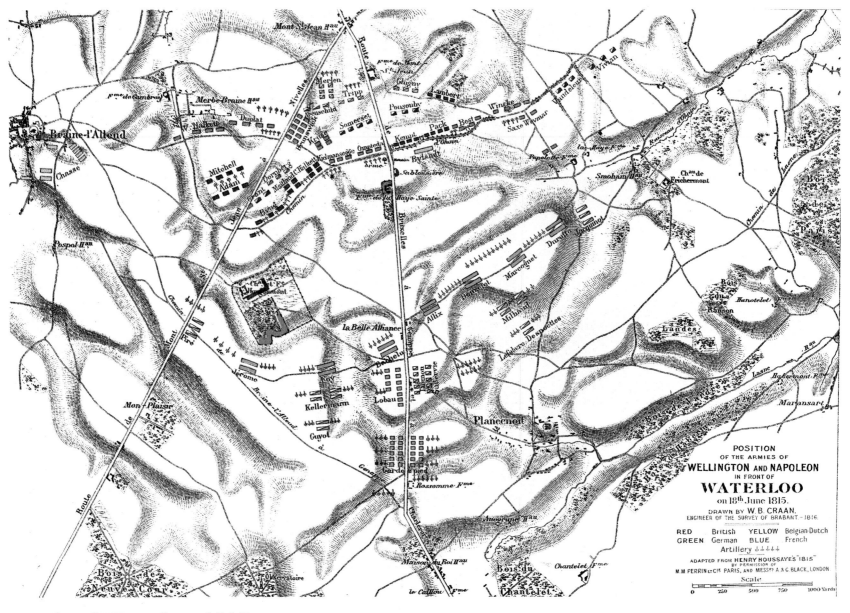

POSITION
OF THE ARMIES OF
WELLINGTON AND NAPOLEON
IN FRONT OF
WATERLOO
on 18th June 1815.
DRAWN BY W.B. CRAAN.
ENGINEER OF THE SURVEY OF BRABANT. - 1816.

RED British YELLOW Belgian-Dutch
GREEN German BLUE French
Artillery ⚔ ⚔ ⚔ ⚔

ADAPTED FROM HENRY HOUSSAYES "1815"
BY PERMISSION OF
M.M. PERRIN et Cie PARIS, AND MESSrs A. & C. BLACK, LONDON.

Scale
0   250   500   750   1000 Yards

Battle of Waterloo, 1815

At Ligny things had gone much better. Napoleon had defeated the Prussians and driven them from the field, leaving 16,000 casualties behind them. One of those casualties was Blücher himself, who had been unhorsed and was helped away from the field by an aide. It was just as well for the Allies he survived, for he was able to countermand the plan of Gneisenau, his principal lieutenant, to retreat to Liège. Nevertheless, Napoleon had won the day: albeit that Ney's lethargy had meant that the Prussian troops had not been as badly beaten as Napoleon had hoped. The next step was to defeat Wellington, whose forces were retreating back down the Brussels road from Quatre Bras toward the ridge of Mont St Jean,

and what would become the battlefield of Waterloo. It is surprising that they were allowed to do so without hindrance, and Napoleon waited until 14:00 on the 17th before kick-starting the pursuit. Wellington's rearguard—ably commanded by the Earl of Uxbridge, FM Henry Paget (1768–1854)—held off the pursuit, and to make matters worse for the French heavy rain soon turned the small country roads into a quagmire. At 18:30 Napoleon reached La Belle Alliance, an inn on the road. "Have all the troops take their positions, we'll see what happens in the morning," he said. This map shows the positions of the armies in front of Waterloo on 18 June.

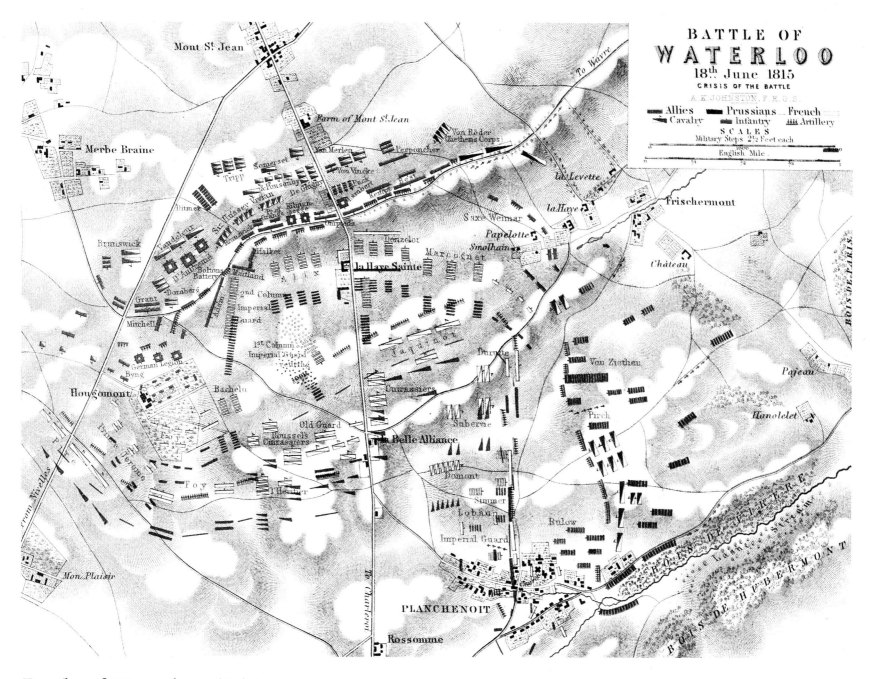

Battle of Waterloo, 1815

The story of the battle of Waterloo is well known. Wellington had chosen his positions with his customary brilliance. His troops were able to use the reverse slope to keep out of direct enemy artillery fire; the French had to attack uphill, and their cavalry were not able to break the Allied squares. The defense of the Chateau de Hougoumont on the right of the Allied line and La Haie Sainte in the center delayed the French. There were many crucial moments, none less than when Uxbridge's heavy cavalry charged and defeated General Dubois's cavalry. In the end the grit of Wellington's men held the field for long enough for Blücher to arrive in the nick of time and carry the day, as can be seen on this map.

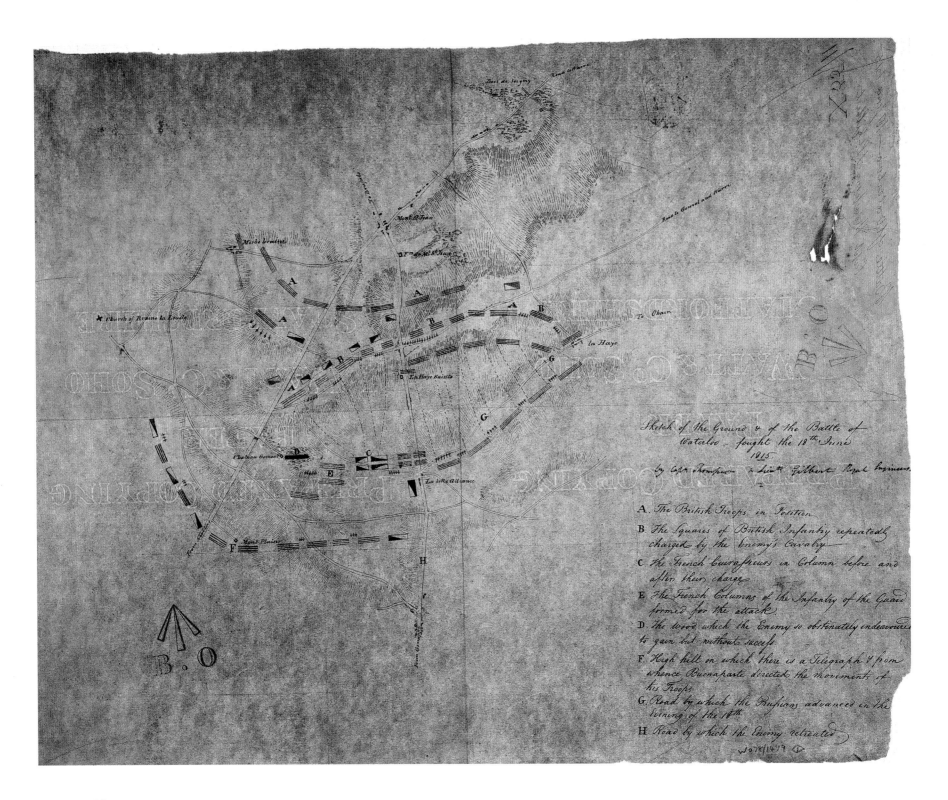

Sketch of the Ground & of the Battle of
Waterloo – fought the 18th June
1815.
by Capt. Thompson & Lieut. Gilbert Royal Engineers.

A. The British Troops in Position

B. The Squares of British Infantry repeatedly
charged by the Enemy's Cavalry

C. The French Cuirassiers in Column before and
after their charge

E. The French Columns of the Infantry of the Guard
formed for the attack

D. The wood which the Enemy so obstinately endeavoured
to gain but without success

F. High hill on which there is a Telegraph & from
whence Buonaparte directed the movements of
his Troops

G. Road by which the Prussians advanced in the
Evening of the 18th

H. Road by which the Enemy retreated

136

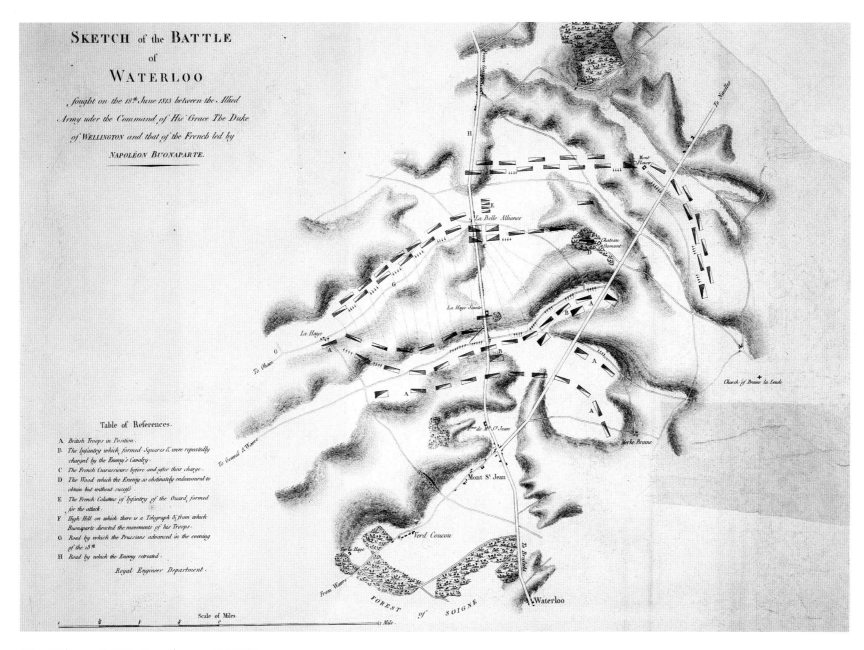

SKETCH of the BATTLE
of
WATERLOO

fought on the 18th June 1815 between the Allied
Army uder the Command of His Grace The Duke
of WELLINGTON and that of the French led by
NAPOLÉON BUONAPARTE.

Table of References.

A   British Troops in Position.
B   The Infantry which formed Squares & were repeatedly
    charged by the Enemy's Cavalry.
C   The French Cuirassiers before and after their charge.
D   The Wood which the Enemy so obstinately endeavoured to
    obtain but without success.
E   The French Columns of Infantry of the Guard formed
    for the attack.
F   High Hill on which there is a Telegraph & from which
    Buonaparte directed the movements of his Troops.
G   Road by which the Prussians advanced in the evening
    of the 18th
H   Road by which the Enemy retreated.

Royal Engineer Department.

Scale of Miles.

Battle of Waterloo, 1815

Left: Sketch of the ground and of the battle of Waterloo by Captain Thompson
and Lt Gilbert RE. The key gives the details of the battle. Note British and Allied
troops in red at the top of the map.
Above: In effect an identical map by the RE department but presented 180
degrees differently with British in red at the bottom of the map.

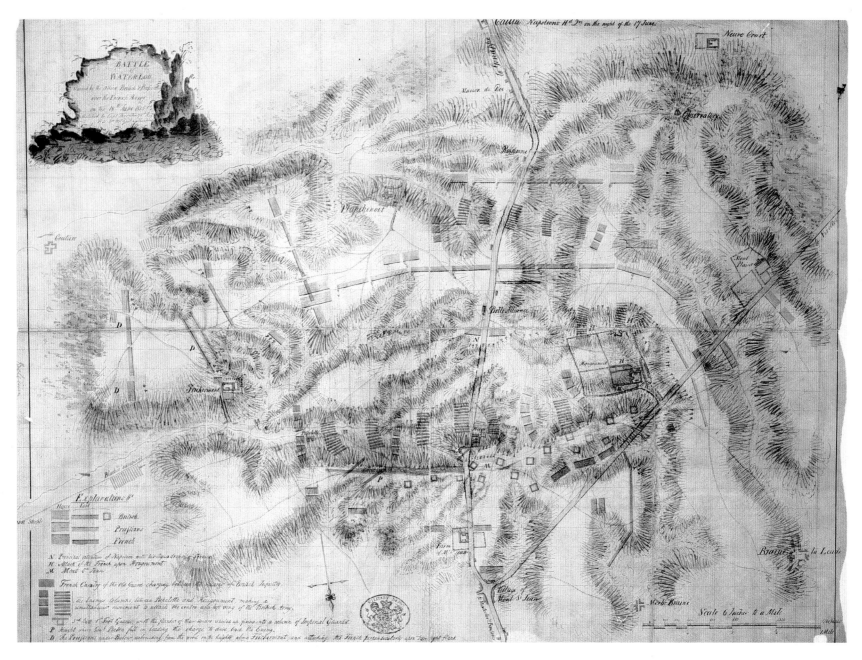

Battle of Waterloo, 1815

Above: An extremely detailed map with extensive notes and keys showing the battle culminating in Blücher's arrival. This was produced by the RM Academy on the anniversary of the battle in 1834.

Right: Interesting version prepared from a sketch by Capt Thornton Deputy Assistant Quartermaster General. Note the French cavalry and the British squares, the Prussians at right under Bülow and the place where Picton fell while straightening the line, just before Uxbridge's cavalry charge.

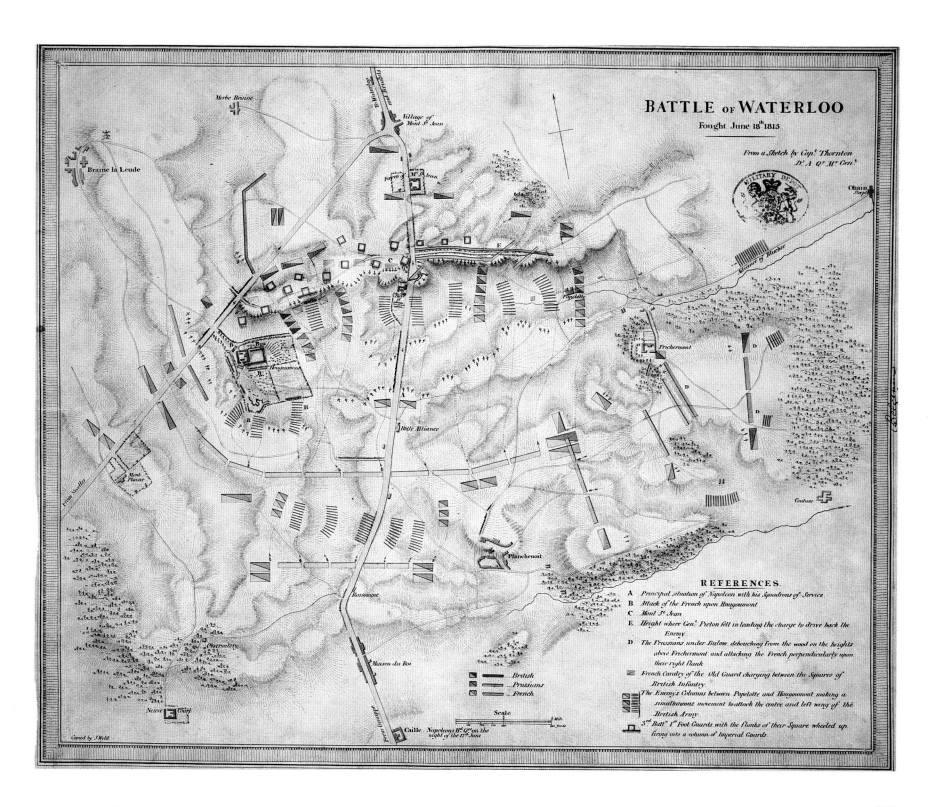

BATTLE OF WATERLOO

Fought June 18th 1815

From a Sketch by Capt. Thornton
Dt. A Qr Mr Genl.

Merbe Braine

Braine la Leude

Village of
Mont St Jean

Farm of Mt St Jean

Obain
Stayple

Advance of Blucher

Frichermont

Hougoumont

Papelotte

Belle Alliance

From Nivelles

Mont
Plaisir

Planchenoit

Rossomme

Couture

Observatory

Maison du Roi

From Genappe

Neuve Court

Scale

Caille . Napoleons Hd Qrs on the
night of the 17th June

Copied by J Weld

REFERENCES.

A   Principal situation of Napoleon with his Squadrons of Service.

B   Attack of the French upon Hougoumont.

C   Mont St Jean.

E   Height where Genl Picton fell in leading the charge to drive back the
    Enemy.

D   The Prussians under Bulow, debouching from the wood on the heights
    above Frichermont and attacking the French perpendicularly upon
    their right flank.

    French Cavalry of the Old Guard charging between the Squares of
    British Infantry.

    The Enemy's Columns between Papelotte and Hougoumont making a
    simultaneous movement to attack the centre and left wing of the
    British Army.

    3rd Battn 1st Foot Guards with the flanks of their Square wheeled up
    firing into a column of Imperial Guards.

British

Prussians

French

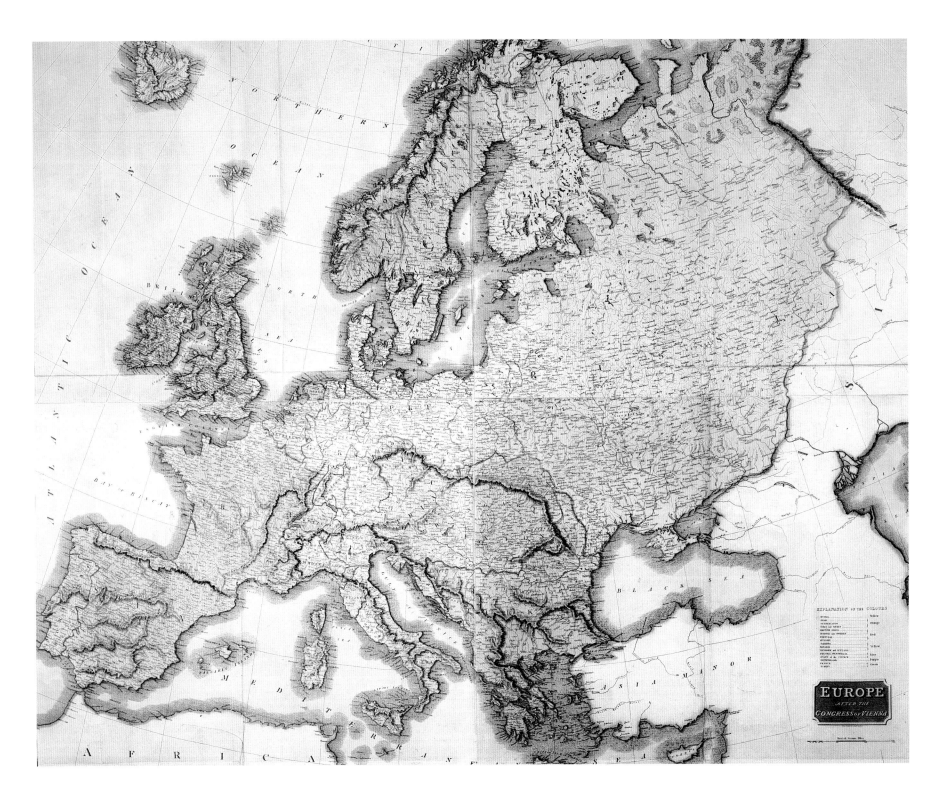

EXPLANATION OF THE COLOURS

EUROPE
AFTER THE
CONGRESS OF VIENNA

140

PARTITIONS OF POLAND

CENTRAL & SOUTH EASTERN EUROPE.
TO ILLUSTRATE VIENNA CONGRESS TREATY.

Europe after the Congress of Vienna, 1816

Left: Following Waterloo, the Congress of Vienna returned to its deliberations and rewriting of borders. This map shows an overview of the end result.

Above: The partitions of Poland in 1772, 1793, 1795 are shown graphically in this map. The pink line shows 1772 boundary; the green line the truncated boundary after the Congress of Vienna. The colored key shows the divisions to Russia (pink), Prussia (green), Austria (yellow)

Right: Winners and losers at the Congress of Vienna: 1 Russia, 2 Poland, 3 Austro-Hungary, 4 Prussia, 5 France, 6 Switzerland, 7 Piedmont, 8 Bavaria, 9 Württemberg, 10 Baden, 11 Holland, 12 Turkey, 13 Hannover, 14 Oldenburg, 15 Saxony, 16 Great Britain, 17 Denmark, 18 Sweden, 19 Venice, 20 Milan, 21 Genoa, 22 Salzburg, 23 Sion, 24 Austrian Netherlands and Liege, 25 Ragusa, 26 Munster. The black lines show the frontiers in 1792.

Northern France, 1815

Following Waterloo the armies of Wellington and Blücher chased Napoleon and his vanquished army toward Paris. Napoleon had hoped to rally them at Genappe: he couldn't and his reign was almost over. The cost of the battles around Waterloo since the 15th was enormous: the French lost 60,000 in the period (including deserters); the Allies 55,000. David Chandler in his excellent book on the battle brings these enormous figures into focus: of 840 British infantry officers, half were killed or wounded. The 12th Light Dragoons, whose memorial is in Waterloo church, had three captains, five lieutenants, nine NCOs and 75 privates killed. After the battle, the fighting was not over. Indeed, as the Allies advanced on Paris they had to leave so many troops behind to watch French garrisons and to maintain their supply lines that they were outnumbered by the time they reached the capital. But Napoleon's time had gone; Louis XVIII would be recalled (he returned to Paris on 8 July) and the Prussians would occupy the country—as is shown in this map of the lines of occupation.

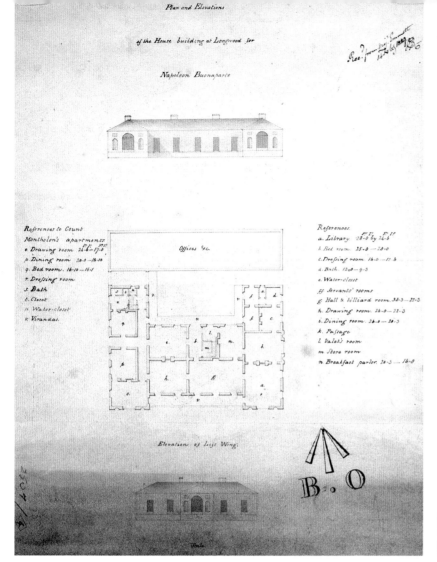

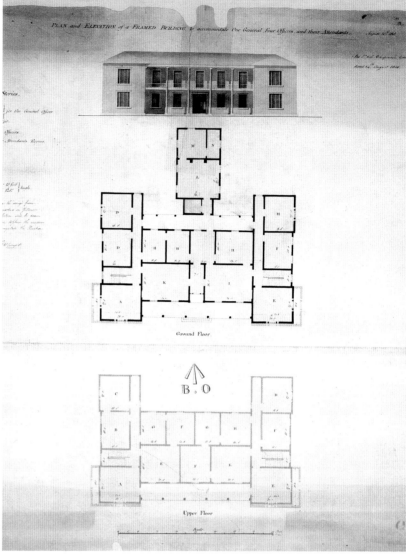

St Helena, 1819

After the defeat at Waterloo, Napoleon signed a second abdication agreement at the Elysée Palace on 22 June 1815. Finally allowed to leave Paris, he evaded the clutches of the Prussians and harbored hopes of getting to America. He reached the west coast of France on 8 July but realized that he would not be allowed across the Atlantic. On 15 July he surrendered himself to Captain Maitland of HMS *Bellerophon*, requesting that asylum would be granted him in England.

It was not to be. On 31 July the *Bellerophon* reached Plymouth, and Napoleon was told of his final destination: St Helena off Africa. A week later he and his retinue embarked on the *Northumberland* bound for St Helena. On 14 October 1815 they arrived in Jamestown Bay. Napoleon disembarked two nights later and he and his retinue waited for some weeks before Longwood House was ready. The British were worried about rescue attempts and beefed up the military presence on the island. Even Tristan Da Cunha, 1,200 miles to the south, was garrisoned. Napoleon died on 5 May 1821. He was buried in a simple grave on the island, but his body was removed on 16 October 1840 and now lies in Les Invalides, Paris.

These drawings show plans of Longwood.

Above left:
A Library
B Bedroom
C Dressing room
D Bath
E WC
F Servants' rooms
G Hall and billiard room
H Drawing room
I Dining room
K Passage
L Valet's room
M Storeroom
N Breakfast parlor

Above right:
A Sitting room
B Bedroom
C Dressing room
D Attendants' rooms
E Sitting rooms
F Bedrooms for officers
G Dressing rooms or attendants' rooms
H Attendants' rooms
I Dining room
K Drawing room
L Kitchen
M Scullery
N Pantry

*IN*DEX OF MAPS